Penguin Books

Utterly Trivial

Utterly Trivial Knowledge:
The Royalty Game

Vida Adamoli

Penguin Books

Penguin Books Ltd, Harmondsworth, Middlesex, England
Viking Penguin Inc., 40 West 23rd Street, New York, New York 10010, USA
Penguin Books Australia Ltd, Ringwood, Victoria, Australia
Penguin Books Canada Ltd, 2801 John Street, Markham, Ontario, Canada L3R 1B4
Penguin Books (NZ) Ltd, 182–190 Wairau Road, Auckland 10, New Zealand

First published 1987

Filmset in 9/10 Century by
Rowland Phototypesetting Ltd
Bury St Edmunds, Suffolk
Printed in Great Britain by
Cox and Wyman Ltd, Reading, Berks

Introduction

My interest in the Royal Family dates from the time in the early seventies when I saw the Queen's knickers. I remember how my eyes popped with thrilled disbelief as I opened an Italian gossip rag and found myself staring at a sneaked photograph of Her Majesty relaxing on a lawn with Princess Margaret, showing several inches of (silk?) undergarment. It was a revelation in every sense of the word. Up until that moment she had been as remote to me as a storybook queen – a dull and dowdy one at that. Now a flash of what should have been censored made her suddenly and deliciously real.

And so, after years of arrogant indifference, I joined millions of others hooked on the greatest and longest-running soap opera in the world. From Rome where I was living at the time, I devoured every scrap of trivia concerning the Royal Family's private lives that regularly appeared in the Italian press – subsequently (and sadly) I found out that nine-tenths of it were untrue.

We Brits have a complicated relationship with our Royals, reverently respectful on the one hand and aggressively proprietorial on the other. Because they belong to us, we hold opinions and pass judgements on every aspect of their lives, hoarding the sort of useless information usually of interest only when it concerns our own family. Knowing the name of the colour rinse the Queen uses on her hair, for example, or what unromantic illness the Queen Mother contracted on her honeymoon, or which member of the Royal Family has a sister who was anorexic, gives us the satisfying illusion of possessing a piece of their lives.

Researching this book I became a Royal bore, unable to restrain myself from tossing out golden nuggets such as how Lord Snowdon had been having an affair with Lucy Lindsay-Hogg before the separation from Margaret was made official, or how George V liked his trousers pressed. I was encouraged, however, by the rapt interest I almost always received from my listeners. As an 'expert in the know', I was frequently asked to verify salacious gossip and treated to countless authoritative statements of the 'it's obvious Diana's fraught relationship with the Queen is destroying her marriage' kind. I came to the conclusion that nobody is completely impervious

to the Royal Mystique – especially after a distinguished
nuclear physicist cornered me at a party to hold forth on the
Queen Mum's taste in hats!

The questions numbered one to six correspond to six cat-
egories which sometimes, inevitably, overlap. They are:

1. THE QUEEN HERSELF

These questions all concern the Queen and her private life
from babyhood on: her wardrobe, her dogs, her likes and
dislikes.

2. THE ROYAL FAMILY

This incorporates all the Queen's living relatives from little
Prince Harry to Princess Michael of Kent.

3. PUBLIC LIFE

This category deals with the official face of royalty: when it
goes splendidly right or shamingly wrong.

4. LOVE AND MARRIAGE

Courtship, marriage, affairs and scandals. Mainly current
ones, but there are some historical tit-bits too.

5. HISTORICAL

History starts at George VI – and works backwards through
the centuries.

6. ABROAD

This is our Royal Family on tours and holidays, as well as
questions about foreign royalty.

Note: Out of respect for the Queen there is no question relating
to her knickers: however you will find questions (and answers)
about the undergarments of some of her lesser relatives.

1

1. What colour rinse does the Queen use on her hair?
2. What music always accompanies the royal breakfasts?
3. When was the famous *Royal Family* film shown?
4. What did the five-year-old Queen Mother give her future husband at their first meeting?
5. For whom was the christening gown worn by all royal babies of recent times made?
6. At which foreign airport was film actress Merle Oberon waiting to greet Prince Philip with a kiss?

76

1. Who said to the Queen, 'Oh, I'm sorry, I didn't recognize you without your crown?'
2. Prince Philip had four sisters. How many brothers did he have?
3. What was the total cost of State funding of the monarchy in 1986?
4. Which was the most publicized of Lord Snowdon's extra-marital affairs?
5. Which royal residence once boasted a bear pit?
6. Who said, 'The Queen is never so happy as when she's being welcomed by a crowd of tribal dancers in grass skirts'?

151

1. Who are the Queen's jewellers?
2. Who described royalty as 'a gold filling in a mouth full of decay'?
3. Which was the first member of the Royal Family to be appointed Warden of the Cinque Ports?
4. What year did Prince Andrew's relationship with Koo Stark end?
5. Who said of the abdication crisis, 'This is a pretty kettle of fish'?
6. What gift did the Queen receive from the South African people when she celebrated her coming of age in their country?

1

1. Chocolate Kiss.
2. Bagpipes.
3. 21 June 1969.
4. The crystallized cherry from her cake.
5. The children of Queen Victoria.
6. Mexico City.

76

1. Lady Diana Cooper.
2. None.
3. Around £15 million.
4. His affair with Lady Jacqueline Rufus-Isaacs.
5. Sandringham.
6. Auberon Waugh.

151

1. Garrard's.
2. John Osborne in 1957.
3. The Queen Mother.
4. 1984.
5. Queen Mary.
6. A necklace of twenty-one perfect diamonds.

2

1. Why did the Queen, as a child, pour a bottle of ink over her head?
2. What was not quite royal about Prince Philip's birth?
3. Who said, 'The car has become the most destructive plaything man has ever known'?
4. Which royal said, 'Marriage is finding someone you can share a flat with'?
5. What was the first question George V asked Lindberg after his solo flight across the Atlantic?
6. Who was fifty-sixth in line of succession to the British throne in 1982?

77

1. At what time are the Queen's corgies served their chopped liver?
2. What was the nickname given to Diana by her flatmates?
3. Which member of the Royal Family reviewed Harry Secombe's novel *Twice Brightly* for Punch?
4. How many kings, queens, princes and princesses attended the Queen's wedding breakfast?
5. Who called Windsor Castle the 'most romantic castle in the world'?
6. What secret did the Queen confide to the Canadian prime minister on her 1959 tour?

152

1. How old was the Queen when she mastered the royal curtsey
2. How did Charles and Anne break their noses?
3. When were the last débutante presentations?
4. Where and when did Peter Townsend and Princess Margaret first admit to being in love?
5. Which Queen lined her coronation robe with rabbit instead of ermine to save expense?
6. Which foreign sovereigns unnerved the Queen when they ignored protocol and dropped in on her unannounced at the Royal Lodge, Windsor?

2

1. She was fed up with her French lesson.
2. He was delivered on the dining room table.
3. Prince Charles.
4. Princess Michael of Kent.
5. 'What did you do about peeing?'
6. HRH Prince Nikola of Yugoslavia.

77

1. At 4 p.m.
2. 'The Landlady'.
3. Prince Charles.
4. Five kings, eight queens, eight princes and ten princesses.
5. Samuel Pepys in 1666.
6. That she hoped she was expecting her third child.

152

1. Not yet two.
2. Charles broke his nose playing rugby, Anne falling off a horse.
3. 1958.
4. In Windsor Castle's red drawing room in the New Year of 1953.
5. Queen Alexandra.
6. The King and Queen of Thailand.

3

1. Who makes the Queen's shoes?
2. Which royal spent much of her childhood in a rented house on the Sandringham estate?
3. What restored Princess Anne's tarnished image in the eyes of the British media?
4. What did Fergie have to give up on her engagement to Prince Andrew?
5. How long did the Duke of Windsor reign as Edward VIII?
6. What was the Queen's remark on being pelted with eggs during her 1986 tour of New Zealand?

78

1. Who was the respected Sandringham resident known to the Queen as 'Royal Zobo'?
2. When did a fully dressed Princess Anne join a crowd of nude dancers?
3. What was Prince Andrew's début as a photographer?
4. Who did Charles wink at when he walked down the aisle at his wedding?
5. Why did the Royal Family change its name to Windsor?
6. Which present member of the Royal Family married a Danish commoner?

153

1. Name the Queen's two favourite journals as a child?
2. What are the shoe sizes of the Queen, Princess Margaret and the Queen Mother?
3. How big is the park of Buckingham Palace?
4. What did the Queen's private secretary say to Townsend on learning of his love affair with Margaret?
5. Which famous architect's father was Dean of Windsor between 1635–59?
6. Where did Prince Philip's parents marry?

3

1. Edward Rayne.
2. Princess Diana.
3. Her work on behalf of the Save the Children Fund.
4. She had to give up her BMW for a British car.
5. Ten months and twenty-one days.
6. She said she preferred her 'New Zealand eggs for breakfast'.

78

1. A prize cow with a record milk yield.
2. When she joined members of the audience on the stage at the end of the nude musical *Hair*.
3. His pictures for the 1985 Ilford Calender.
4. Marina Ogilvy.
5. Because George V's German name provoked rumours that he was pro-German.
6. Prince Richard, Duke of Gloucester.

153

1. *Punch* and the *Children's Newspaper*.
2. Size 5, size 4, size 4½.
3. Nearly 800 acres.
4. 'You must be either mad or bad.'
5. Christopher Wren's father.
6. Darmstadt, capital of Hesse.

4

1. When was the only time the Queen signed an autograph for a member of the public?
2. How many girls joined Princess Anne for school lessons at the Palace?
3. How many prime ministers have served under the Queen?
4. Which hospital did both Anne and Diana choose to have their babies?
5. Which monarch refused to believe such a thing as lesbianism could exist?
6. Who said, 'Australia got me over my shyness'?

79

1. What is the Queen's only health problem?
2. Who's decision was it to send all the Queen's sons to Gordonstoun?
3. What was the Queen Mother's first public engagement after ninety-six days of deep mourning for George VI?
4. Who assured the world that Diana 'has had no lovers'?
5. How did Queen Victoria inscribe the copy of her book she gave to Dickens?
6. How did Princess Alexandra praise Mexico?

154

1. What is *Private Eye*'s satirical nickname for the Queen?
2. Which member of the Royal Family is a qualified architect?
3. Of how many regiments and corps is the Queen Colonel-in-Chief?
4. With whom did Princess Margaret become emotionally involved when Snowdon was away on a long assignment?
5. What did George VI say when knighting his physician, Professor Learmouth?
6. When and where was Prince Charles's first visit to a Communist country?

4

1. In 1945 for female Sergeant Pat Hayes.
2. Two.
3. Eight.
4. St Mary's Hospital, Paddington.
5. Queen Victoria.
6. Prince Charles.

79

1. Sinusitis.
2. Prince Philip's.
3. She inspected the battalion of the Black Watch.
4. Her uncle, Lord Fermoy.
5. 'From the humblest of writers to one of the greatest'.
6. 'This country makes me gasp. And it isn't only the altitude.'

154

1. Brenda.
2. Prince Richard, Duke of Gloucester.
3. Over fifty.
4. Antony Burton, Lady Sarah's godfather.
5. 'You used a knife on me, now I'm going to use one on you!'
6. 1978, Yugoslavia.

5

1. Why did the Queen visit a spiritual healer in 1970?
2. Who said, 'I have as much privacy as a goldfish in a bowl'?
3. How often does the Queen meet to talk with her prime minister?
4. Who were Princess Anne's page and bridesmaid?
5. Which organization used Clarence House as offices during World War II?
6. What was Princess Margaret's first solo trip abroad?

80

1. What is the total amount of holiday taken by the Queen each year?
2. Name three sets of injuries sustained by Princess Anne while riding?
3. What is the correct pronunciation of 'Ma'am'?
4. What is the most unenviable private aspect of the Queen's life?
5. What makes Princess Anne's son extra special?
6. Who were the first reigning monarchs to stay on American soil?

155

1. Name four everyday items that bear the Queen's royal cipher?
2. What does the Queen Mother call her horses?
3. When was the surname Mountbatten-Windsor first used on an official document?
4. What unromantic illness did the Queen Mother catch on her honeymoon?
5. How much was the expert French swordsman paid to execute Anne Boleyn?
6. How many countries were present at the first Commonwealth Conference of the Queen's reign?

5

1. To treat an inflamed tendon.
2. Princess Margaret.
3. Once a week.
4. Prince Edward and Lady Sarah Armstrong-Jones.
5. The Red Cross.
6. A private visit to Italy for a month in 1949.

80

1. Between eighteen and nineteen weeks.
2. A broken nose, a bruised shoulder and thigh, cracked vertebra and concussion.
3. 'Marm'.
4. She alone has to make the decisions about the romances of close relatives.
5. He is the first royal baby to be born a commoner for over 500 years.
6. George VI and the Queen Mother during their 1937 State visit of America and Canada.

155

1. Her personal kettle, her butter pats, her cheques, her milkbottles.
2. Her 'darling boys'.
3. On the register signed by Princess Anne on her marriage.
4. Whooping cough.
5. £23.
6. Eight.

6

1. Where are the Queen's dogs buried?
2. Why did Princess Margaret have plastic surgery?
3. Who asked the Queen why women were required to wear gloves to meet her and not men?
4. Why were Margaret and the Duchess of Kent unable to attend Prince Edward's christening?
5. Which queen was pregnant twenty times?
6. Why was there nobody to greet the Queen when she landed at Dubrovnik for an official visit?

81

1. What is the Queen's connection with George Washington?
2. Why did the owner of a tea shop refuse to sell cakes to the newly married Sarah Ferguson?
3. What parts of Windsor Castle are open to the public?
4. How old was the Queen when she had her last child?
5. What unfulfilled desire did old Queen Mary confess to the Queen Mother?
6. Where and with whom did the Queen go into the tunnel of love?

156

1. Where are the Queen's racing pigeons housed?
2. Who said, 'I am not a member of the Royal Family, I am married to a member of the Royal Family'?
3. Where is the Service of the Garter held?
4. When and where did Anne first meet Mark Phillips?
5. How did Ellen Terry describe Queen Victoria's singing voice?
6. What did the Queen refuse a little Australian girl on her 1981 visit?

6

1. Near the summerhouse at Sandringham.
2. To remove her double chin.
3. Barbra Streisand, at the 1975 screening of *Funny Girl*.
4. They'd just given birth themselves.
5. Queen Anne (she miscarried frequently and most of the babies that were born died of hydrocephalus in infancy).
6. The welcoming committee had been told that her plane had been diverted to Titograd.

81

1. He's her sixth cousin twice removed.
2. Failing to recognize her, he said they didn't do take-away.
3. Apartments in the Upper Ward, Queen Mary's Doll's House and the exhibition of drawings.
4. Thirty-eight.
5. She said, 'There's one thing I never did and wish I had done: climbed over a fence.'
6. Denmark, with Prince Henrick.

156

1. At their trainer's semi-detached in King's Lynn.
2. Lord Snowdon.
3. The Chapel of St George, Windsor Castle.
4. In 1968, at a reception in the Whitbread wine cellar in the City.
5. 'A silver stream flowing over golden stones'.
6. A kiss.

7

1. What are the usual contents of the Queen's handbag?
2. Which royal decorator was asked by Charles and Diana to redesign Highgrove?
3. Which royal sailed into the wrong cocktail party at a Mayfair Hotel?
4. What was the date of the Queen and Prince Philip's wedding?
5. Which is the oldest order of knighthood in the world?
6. How old was King Carl XVI Gustaf of Sweden when he came to the throne?

82

1. What is the Queen reported to have done when she first saw her full coronation rig?
2. When Prince Philip said he was a practitioner of the 'science of dontopedology', what did he mean?
3. What was the six-year-old Queen's first official engagement?
4. Which was the Queen Mother's first married home?
5. Who said George VI had 'no wit, no learning, no humour, except of a rather schoolboy brand'?
6. Who said, 'When I die India will be found engraved on my heart'?

157

1. What does the Queen do if she spills salt?
2. When do the Royal Family traditionally exchange their Christmas presents?
3. When did Prince Charles make his first official appearance at Royal Ascot?
4. What was the significance of the engagement ring Tony designed for Margaret?
5. Who was the last monarch to be born abroad?
6. Where did Prince Philip walk out of a press conference without uttering a word?

7

1. A small compact, a lipstick, a hanky and, occasionally, a set of car keys.
2. David Hicks.
3. The Queen Mother.
4. 20 November 1947.
5. The Order of the Garter.
6. Twenty-seven.

82

1. Overwhelmed, she burst into tears.
2. That he habitually 'opened his mouth and put his foot in it'.
3. She opened the Princess Elizabeth Hostel in Highgate.
4. White Lodge in Richmond Park.
5. Chips Channon.
6. Queen Mary.

157

1. She throws it over her left shoulder.
2. On Christmas Eve.
3. June 1968.
4. The ruby set like a rosebud within a diamond marguerite is a play on her name, Margaret Rose.
5. George I.
6. La Guardia, New York.

8

1. What stands now on the site of the house in Bruton Street where the Queen was born?
2. Why has Lord Snowdon got one leg an inch shorter than the other?
3. Who is Colonel-in-Chief of the 14th/20th King's Hussars?
4. Which great duke's daughter was tipped as Charles's possible bride?
5. The Queen is the 42nd Sovereign of England since William the Conqueror. How many queens have reigned before her?
6. Which monarch held the record for the biggest breakfast ever served at the Connaught Hotel in London?

83

1. Which dances does the Queen excel at?
2. What was Prince Philip's official religion before his marriage?
3. Which royal made a TV film called *Pilot Royal*?
4. How many bridesmaids did the Queen have?
5. What is the legend of the Koh-i-Noor diamond?
6. When did the Queen finally get to visit her husband's sisters in their own homes?

158

1. When the Queen was born what was her position in line of succession to the throne?
2. Which member of the Royal Family has a sister who was an anorexic?
3. What was the date of the Queen's coronation?
4. How long had Snowdon been having an affair with Lucy Lindsay-Hogg before his official separation from Margaret?
5. Which monarch instituted the Maundy ceremony?
6. Who calls Prince Philip 'Number-one-fellah-belong-missus-Queen'?

8

1. The Lombard North Central Bank.
2. He contracted polio while at Eton.
3. Princess Anne.
4. The daughter of the Duke of Wellington, Jane Wellesley.
5. Five, she is the sixth Sovereign Queen.
6. The famous glutton King Farouk I of Egypt.

83

1. Tap dancing and the twist.
2. Greek Orthodox.
3. Prince Charles.
4. Eight.
5. It's a woman's diamond and will bring misfortune and early death to any man who possesses it.
6. During her 1965 State Visit to Federal Germany.

158

1. Third.
2. Diana.
3. 2 June 1953.
4. Fourteen months.
5. Edward I.
6. The natives of Papua New Guinea.

9

1. Who are Smokey, Shadow, Spark, Myth, Fable and Diamond?
2. By what affectionate nickname is the Queen Mother called by her grandchildren?
3. When did the Queen first ride in state up the Mall?
4. When did the Queen and Prince Philip celebrate their silver wedding anniversary?
5. Name six reputedly homosexual kings.
6. Which royal was made a Red Indian chieftain with the title 'His Royal Highness Prince Red Crow'?

84

1. What length does the Queen keep her hemlines?
2. Who has been dubbed 'Action Man'?
3. When was the Duke of Edinburgh's Awards established?
4. Why was Princess Margaret not allowed to marry Townsend?
5. What was the profession of Richard Podelicote, who masterminded the plot to steal the Crown Jewels in 1303?
6. Where did the Queen and Prince Philip live when she was a Navy wife in Malta?

159

1. Who are the Queen's bankers?
2. Which of his sons has Philip described as 'a natural boss'?
3. How much did the royal yacht *Britannia* cost to build?
4. Why was the Queen Mother thrilled at the day chosen for Prince William's christening?
5. What prompted George V to say, 'I thought chaps like that shot themselves'?
6. Where did Prince Philip quip, 'You have mosquitoes, we have the press'?

9

1. The Queen's corgies.
2. Granny Royal.
3. At the age of eleven on the occasion of her father's Coronation.
4. 20 November 1972.
5. William II, Richard I, Edward II, Richard II, James I, William III.
6. Prince Charles.

84

1. One and a half inches below the knee.
2. Prince Charles.
3. 1961.
4. Because he was divorced.
5. He was a travelling salesman.
6. Villa Guardamangia.

159

1. Coutts & Co.
2. Prince Andrew.
3. £2 million.
4. It was her eighty-second birthday.
5. The discovery that an elderly acquaintance was a homosexual.
6. In Dominica.

10

1. Which prime minister said the Queen has 'the heart and stomach of a man'?
2. Which Royal did a crash course in French at the Berlitz School?
3. When did the Queen initiate informal luncheons at the Palace to meet a wider selection of her people?
4. When did Queen Victoria say, 'It's like taking a poor lamb to be sacrificed'?
5. Which royal order has a risqué legend attached to its origin?
6. What did the Queen wear to open the Australian Parliament during her 1953–4 Commonwealth tour.

85

1. Name the three couturiers the Queen has favoured.
2. Which royal home has been described as looking like a 'railway hotel'?
3. What did Augustus John reply when ordered to arrive 'dead sober' to paint the Queen?
4. About which well-suited couple did the Queen Mother say they could have been computer-dated?
5. Which monarch created the Duchy of Cornwall?
6. Which member of the Royal Family had a brother-in-law who was an officer in the Gestapo?

160

1. How much does the Queen weigh?
2. Who said of photographers, 'All those chaps want is to catch you picking your nose'?
3. What produce does Balmoral sell?
4. Who was the Duke of Windsor's black girlfriend?
5. Name four ghosts that haunt Windsor Castle.
6. Where and when was Prince Charles's first trip abroad?

10

1. Harold Macmillan.
2. Princess Anne.
3. In 1956.
4. On the marriage of her eldest daughter to the future Emperor of Prussia.
5. The Order of the Garter.
6. Her coronation gown.

85

1. Hartnell, Hardy Amies and Ian Thomas.
2. Sandringham.
3. 'Must I be dead sober when I leave?'
4. Princess Anne and Mark Phillips.
5. Edward III in 1337.
6. Prince Philip.

160

1. Around 8 stone.
2. Prince Philip.
3. Grouse, venison and game-fish.
4. Singer Florence Mills.
5. George III, Elizabeth I, Anne Boleyn and Herne the Hunter.
6. He visited his paternal aunts in Germany in 1962.

11

1. Who guards the Queen's bedroom at night?
2. What unflattering nicknames did the Duke of Windsor give the Queen Mother?
3. Who was the first monarch to accede to the throne while up a tree?
4. What did the Queen do with her wedding bouquet?
5. Who receives the money in the Maundy ceremony?
6. How many royal weddings had been held at St Paul's before that of Charles and Diana?

86

1. How old was the Queen when she first went to live in Buckingham Palace?
2. Who said, 'People think it's a miracle a Princess can even read or write'?
3. What information other than that of state is traditionally included in the Queen's dispatch boxes?
4. Where did Tony and Margaret go for their honeymoon?
5. Why must the Coronation ring traditionally have a sapphire?
6. What was the name of the house on Corfu where Prince Philip was born?

161

1. What wonderful gift did the people of Wales give the Queen and her sister when children?
2. Which art school did Lady Sarah Armstrong-Jones attend?
3. When did Prince Charles get his wings?
4. How did Diana keep Prince William quiet during his christening?
5. How did the Queen Mother define her new role after the Abdication?
6. Where and when did Prince Charles grow a beard?

11

1. A uniformed policeman.
2. 'The Monster of Glamis', 'The Dowdy Duchess,' 'That fat Scotch cook'.
3. The Queen.
4. It was placed on the tomb of The Unknown Warrior in Westminster Abbey.
5. As many old men and women as there are in the sovereign's age.
6. None.

86

1. Nearly eleven.
2. Princess Michael.
3. Current scandal concerning rulers, politicians and prominent men and women.
4. The West Indies.
5. The sapphire is a reminder of the sapphire ring given by St Edward to a beggar.
6. 'Mon Repos'.

161

1. A 15-foot-high model Welsh cottage.
2. Camberwell College of Art.
3. August 1977.
4. She gave him her little finger to suck.
5. 'The intolerable honour of being Queen'.
6. In Canada in 1975.

12

1. How old was the Queen when she got her first pony?
2. Which royal has the aristocratic initials E. A. R. L.?
3. How much money was raised by the Silver Jubilee Appeal in 1977?
4. When did the public first suspect Margaret and Townsend were in love?
5. How many albums did George V's valuable stamp collection fill?
6. Who were the first British royals to set foot in Russia since the revolution?

87

1. Why did the Queen go into hospital in 1982?
2. Who said, 'Basically I'm a carpenter'?
3. Which member of the Royal Family is allowed to study State papers with the Queen?
4. How did Roddy Llewellyn address Margaret in public?
5. How many times did the Sebastopol bell at Windsor toll when George VI died?
6. Where did Charles take a holiday immediately after his investiture as Prince of Wales?

162

1. When did the Queen make her first public speech?
2. What is the Queen Mother reputed to have said when her footmen were late bringing her nightcap?
3. How long is the list of likes and dislikes prepared as a guide for people hosting the Queen?
4. How did Diana break with the royal tradition of expectant mums?
5. What did Queen Victoria die of?
6. What foreign visits did the Queen make in her fortieth year?

12

1. Three and a half.
2. Prince Edward Antony Richard Louis.
3. £16 million.
4. When Coronation morning cameras caught Margaret picking fluff off his jacket.
5. 325.
6. Prince Philip and Princess Anne for the European Championships in Kiev.

87

1. To have her wisdom tooth removed.
2. Lord Snowdon.
3. Prince Charles.
4. Ma'am.
5. Fifty-six – one for every day of the King's life.
6. Malta.

162

1. 31 May 1944, on behalf of the NSPCC.
2. 'I don't know what you two old queens are doing down there, but this old Queen is dying of thirst.'
3. 6000 words.
4. Instead of retiring into private life, she kept up a heavy schedule into her sixth month.
5. Cerebral haemorrhage.
6. A tour of the Caribbean and a state visit to Belgium.

13

1. What part did the Queen play in Buckingham Palace's production of Aladdin in 1943?
2. Which member of the Royal Family was treated by a psychiatrist?
3. When did Charles and Anne first attend the State Opening of Parliament?
4. How did Trafalgar Square celebrate Prince Charles's birth?
5. Which Queen was four inches taller than her consort?
6. Which foreign royal personage reputedly had a baby by a servant?

88

1. Who are the Queen's solicitors?
2. What secret lies under Buckingham Palace?
3. Who arranged the Investiture of the Prince of Wales?
4. What words accompanied the wreath the Queen Mother placed on her husband's coffin?
5. How did George V show good will when meeting his first socialist government in 1933?
6. Where did the Queen first wear her spectacles in public?

163

1. Who was the Queen's partner at her first charity ball?
2. Why was Princess Margaret told to give up alcohol for a year?
3. What was Charles doing on the TV programme *Jackanory* in 1984?
4. What was the popular press's nickname for Prince Andrew?
5. When did Elizabeth I refuse the sovereignty of the Netherlands?
6. Where was the Queen kept waiting in a hot desert tent for more than an hour while her host rested in an air-conditioned caravan?

A

13

1. Aladdin.
2. Princess Margaret during the break-up of her marriage.
3. October 1967.
4. The fountains were floodlit blue for a week.
5. Queen Mary was four inches taller than William of Orange.
6. Marie of Mecklenberg.

88

1. Messrs Farrer.
2. A special branch of the London Underground linking the Palace to Heathrow Airport.
3. The Duke of Norfolk and Lord Snowdon.
4. 'Darling Bertie, from his always loving Elizabeth.'
5. He wore a red tie.
6. For the opening of the Canadian Parliament in October 1977.

163

1. Rupert Nevill.
2. She was being treated for alcoholic hepatitis.
3. Reading his own story, *The Old Man of Lochnagar*.
4. 'Randy Andy'.
5. 1575.
6. Morocco, 1980. Her host was King Hassan.

14

1. Which inn sheltered the Queen and her dresser for two hours in a snow blizzard?
2. Who is the Queen Mother's favourite hat designer?
3. In what year did George VI make the newly married Queen and her husband privy councillors?
4. Who was the first royal to kiss his bride in public?
5. How did Queen Victoria describe Balmoral?
6. How much weight did Prince Charles lose on his 1977 tour of the USA?

89

1. Name the Girl Guide Patrol formed at the Palace for the Queen and Margaret.
2. Which famous female singer of the 1940s is a close friend of the Queen Mother.
3. How many official engagements were undertaken by Princess Margaret in 1977.
4. Where did Anne and Mark Phillips spend their wedding night?
5. What did the Queen Mother say after learning to use a revolver in 1940?
6. Which member of the Royal Family had a father imprisoned in Athens on a charge of treason?

164

1. What cooking ingredient has the Queen banned from the royal kitchens?
2. What is Diana's prize jewel?
3. How much mail is dealt with by Buckingham Palace's post office in an average year?
4. When was Armstrong-Jones given the title of Earl of Snowdon?
5. Which Queen reigned for only nine days?
6. Where did the Duke of Windsor reside after the Abdication?

14

1. The Cross Hands at Old Sodbury in Avon.
2. Rudolf.
3. 1951.
4. Edward VII.
5. 'A pretty little castle in the old Scotch style'.
6. A stone.

89

1. The Kingfisher Patrol.
2. Dame Vera Lynn.
3. 177.
4. Princess Alexandra's house in Richmond Park.
5. 'Now I shan't go down like all the others'.
6. Prince Philip.

164

1. Garlic.
2. The diamond lovers' knot and drop-pearl tiara she received as a present from the Queen.
3. Over 75000 items.
4. When Princess Margaret became pregnant.
5. Lady Jane Grey.
6. France.

15

1. What was the name of the Queen's rocking horse when she was a child?
2. Who said, 'I hate royal portraits – so stiff, so boring'?
3. How many acres of land is owned by the Duchy of Cornwall?
4. Who said to the Queen, 'Poor Lil. Nothing of your own, not even your own love affair'?
5. The estimate for building Buckingham Palace was £252,690. How much did it eventually cost?
6. Which monarch said, 'Canada made us'?

90

1. What did the Queen reply when Anne suggested she wear a mini skirt?
2. What message did the Queen Mother send her father when she ran out of money as a girl?
3. Who designed the guest chairs for Prince Charles's Investiture?
4. Where did Prince Philip propose to the Queen?
5. Which king smuggled crown jewels to Amsterdam and sold them at a fraction of their true value?
6. Who were the first members of the Royal Family to sail in the Britannia?

165

1. What was the Queen's opening remark when Michael Noakes came to paint her portrait?
2. Which member of the Royal Family is a notoriously bad speller?
3. Who was the Queen's first official private secretary?
4. Why did Margaret break off her unofficial engagement to Billy Wallace?
5. Which monarch was knighted at twenty-nine days old?
6. How many hands did the Queen shake during her 1953–4 Commonwealth tour?

15

1. Caesar.
2. Princess Michael.
3. 131,744 acres in nine counties.
4. Princess Margaret.
5. More than double.
6. George VI.

90

1. 'I'm not a film star'.
2. 'SOS, LSD, RSVP'.
3. Lord Snowdon and John Pound.
4. Balmoral.
5. Charles I.
6. Prince Charles and Princess Anne.

165

1. 'I really must do something about the curtains'.
2. Prince Philip.
3. John (Jock) Colville.
4. Because he had an affair with another woman.
5. Edward VIII.
6. An estimated 13,000.

16

1. What is the Queen's personal car?
2. Who said, 'I'm one of those ignorant bums that never went to university and a fat lot of harm it did me'?
3. Who was the director of the first Royal Family film?
4. Who said on the wedding morning, 'Today Diana is vowing to help her country for the rest of her life'?
5. How did George VI refer to his stammer?
6. Who was the oldest of the distinguished inhabitants presented to the Queen in Tonga?

91

1. Who does the Queen give plum pudding to at Christmas?
2. Who said, 'I suppose I'll now be known as Charley's Aunt'?
3. Which is the only official ceremony at which the Queen wears a crown and the Robe of State?
4. How much did Charles and Diana's married home, Highgrove House, cost?
5. When were all the baths in Buckingham Palace painted with a five-inch line?
6. What was the reason for the Queen Mother's visit to Munster in West Germany in 1984?

166

1. How many tiaras does the Queen possess?
2. Who are Brian, Yvonne, Keith and Erica?
3. What did the Queen Mother say to her children when their father became king?
4. How long did it take Charles to propose to Diana?
5. What London landmark was originally the gateway to Buckingham Palace?
6. What did the Queen do when a roof collapsed on her in Fiji during the Silver Jubilee Tour?

16

1. A 1971 3.5 litre Rover.
2. Prince Philip.
3. Richard Cawston.
4. Her father, Earl Spencer.
5. 'The curse which God has put on me'.
6. Tuimalila, the great turtle who had met Captain Cook.

91

1. All the members of her staff.
2. Princess Margaret.
3. The State Opening of Parliament.
4. £800,000.
5. During World War II.
6. To tour the British Military Hospital.

166

1. Over twenty.
2. *Private Eye*'s nicknames for Prince Philip, Princess Margaret, Prince Charles and Princess Diana.
3. 'We must make the best of it.'
4. Six months.
5. Marble Arch.
6. She took the opportunity to re-apply her lipstick.

17

1. What did Gordon Richards reply when the Queen congratulated him on winning the Derby?
2. When did Lord Linley get his first pair of water skis?
3. When did the Queen start planning her wardrobe for the Jubilee Tour?
4. How much rent did newly wed Princess Anne and Mark Phillips pay for a rented Georgian house near Sandhurst?
5. For which special person did Southampton dockers break the 1953 Dock Strike?
6. Where and when did Diana receive her first public curtsey?

92

1. Why was the Queen ordered by Windsor's head stable girl to fetch a pail of water?
2. In what year was the attempted kidnap of Princess Anne?
3. What coincidental promotion did Prince Philip receive the day Anne was born?
4. How did Charles ask the Earl of Spencer for Diana's hand?
5. Who hit Queen Victoria over the head with a cane?
6. How many speeches did the Queen make and how many did she listen to on her 1953–4 Canadian tour?

167

1. Who was the Queen's first jockey?
2. Who makes the Queen's kilts?
3. For which TV programme did Prince Philip act as narrator?
4. What are Charles and Diana's compatible sun signs?
5. Who established the tradition of the bagpipes being played at royal breakfasts?
6. How did the Queen answer the advisers who pressed her to cancel her 1961 trip to Ghana because they considered it too risky?

17

1. 'May I congratulate you, your Majesty, on winning the world.'
2. At the age of five.
3. Two years in advance.
4. £8 per week.
5. The Queen Mother.
6. In Gibraltar in August 1981.

92

1. She failed to recognize her.
2. 1974.
3. He was made Lieutenant-Commander and given command of the frigate *Magpie*.
4. He telephoned him.
5. Robert Pat.
6. She made 157 and listened to 276.

167

1. Gordon Richards.
2. Hartnell.
3. *The Restless Sphere*.
4. Scorpio and Cancer.
5. Queen Victoria.
6. 'Nkrumah might invite Khrushchev, and you wouldn't like that, would you?'

18

1. How long was the Queen's private meeting with the Pope at Buckingham Palace?
2. What A-levels did Prince Andrew get?
3. Which member of the Royal Family took part in an episode of *The Archers*.
4. When and where was Roddy officially introduced to the Queen?
5. Why was the Queen Mother glad when Buckingham Palace was bombed in World War II?
6. Where was Prince Charles welcomed by a troop of bare-breasted dancing girls?

93

1. How much schooling did the Queen have each week?
2. Which member of the Royal Family said everything worthwhile has to be 'worked at'?
3. When did Mark Phillips leave the Army?
4. Whose sword did Prince Philip use to cut his wedding cake?
5. What were George V's unofficial last words?
6. What *faux pas* did Diana commit on her 1984 visit to Oslo?

168

1. How old was the Queen when she wore braces on her teeth?
2. Which of Prince Philip's relatives was a student nurse at St Thomas's Hospital?
3. Charles is heir apparent, but when the Queen was a princess she was only heir presumptive. What's the difference?
4. In what year did the Queen Mother get married?
5. How many coronations were celebrated in the twentieth century?
6. Who correctly predicted that Charles was about to become a father two and a half weeks before the official announcement?

18

1. Thirty-five minutes.
2. History, English, Economics with Political Science.
3. Princess Margaret.
4. After church at Windsor.
5. She said, 'It makes me feel I can look the East End in the face.'
6. On his 1984 visit to Papua New Guinea.

93

1. Seven and a half hours.
2. Prince Charles.
3. In the spring of 1978.
4. His grandfather's, Prince Louis of Battenberg.
5. 'Bugger Bognor'.
6. She forgot to turn at the top of the steps to the plane and wave goodbye to her hosts.

168

1. Thirteen.
2. His niece, Princess Margarita of Baden.
3. The Queen's succession was subject to no son being born. As eldest son, Charles's succession is guaranteed.
4. 1923.
5. Four.
6. Graham Latimer, president of New Zealand's Maori Council.

19

1. Where are the Queen's private apartments in Buckingham Palace situated?
2. When did Diana's uncle commit suicide and why?
3. What was Princess Anne's first solo public engagement?
4. What would Margaret have forfeited if she'd married Townsend?
5. Which monarch said, 'Everybody grows but me'?
6. Why did Philip accept $100,000 to swim in a Miami millionaire's pool?

94

1. How old was the Queen when she mistook a remark about Dante the poet for one about Dante the thoroughbred?
2. Which Royal was captain of the hockey team?
3. When did a young Prince Andrew say, 'I do wish mummy would say no sometimes'?
4. Who was Mark Phillips rumoured to be having an affair with in 1981?
5. When did Buckingham Palace pass into royal hands?
6. What title did Grace Kelly acquire when she married Prince Rainier?

169

1. What is the Queen's favourite spa water?
2. What was Augustus John's excuse for failing to turn up for his first portrait session with the Queen Mother?
3. How old was Charles when the Queen made him Knight of the Garter?
4. Who said, 'A boy and then a girl would be perfection'?
5. Which architect was commissioned by George IV to redesign the present Buckingham Palace?
6. What experience marked a turning point in Prince Charles's spiritual development?

19

1. On the first floor overlooking Constitution Hill.
2. 1984. He'd been suffering from depression.
3. Presenting the traditional leeks to the Welsh Guards at Pirbright in 1969.
4. Her royal rights, her duties, her income from the civil list, her right to live in Britain.
5. The eighteen-year-old Queen Victoria.
6. To raise money for the Variety Club of Great Britain.

94

1. Nineteen.
2. Princess Diana.
3. Watching the Queen give formal assent to march off the old colours at Trooping the Colour.
4. Angela Rippon.
5. In 1762.
6. Her Serene Highness the Princess of Monaco.

169

1. Malvern.
2. His telegram said he was 'suffering from the influence'.
3. Ten.
4. The newly married Queen.
5. John Nash.
6. A secret nine-day trek in the African bush.

20

1. Which was the first dress Norman Hartnell designed for the Queen?
2. Why was Prince Andrew carried to bed on the night of the Silver Jubilee Fireworks?
3. Who is Patron of the Royal Ballet?
4. Where was Townsend banished when his affair with Margaret became public?
5. Who said, 'There is only one Jesus Christ and all the rest is a dispute over trifles'?
6. Which was the most poignant event of the royal calendar in 1984?

95

1. Who said, 'When the Queen smiled I could have climbed Everest'?
2. By what nicknames did the Queen's children call their nanny, Mabel Anderson?
3. Who is president of the British Olympic Association?
4. Who called the Duke of Windsor's love for Mrs Simpson 'one of the great loves of history'?
5. What was the last famous bulletin on George V's health?
6. Where did Princess Margaret, feeling cold, refuse to review a regiment and get back into her car?

170

1. What homeopathic remedies does the Queen take for her sinusitis?
2. Which royal greeted the Queen by jumping up and down with a rose in his mouth?
3. How does the Queen manage always to arrive for Trooping the Colour just as the clock strikes eleven?
4. Which was the first royal wedding to be broadcast on radio?
5. Who was the tiniest dwarf ever in royal service?
6. In which country was the Queen treated as an 'honorary gentleman'?

20

1. The bridesmaid dress she wore for the 1935 wedding of the Duke and Duchess of Gloucester.
2. He was drunk.
3. Princess Margaret.
4. To Brussels.
5. Elizabeth I.
6. The commemoration of the D-Day landings in Normandy.

95

1. Harry Secombe after receiving his knighthood.
2. 'Mamba' and 'Masterful Mabel'.
3. Princess Anne.
4. Winston Churchill.
5. 'The King's life is moving peacefully towards its close.'
6. In West Germany in 1980.

170

1. Arsenic, onions and deadly nightshade.
2. Prince Andrew on his return from the Falklands.
3. The clock is put forward or back as required.
4. Prince George, Duke of Kent's wedding to Princess Marina of Greece in 1934.
5. Queen Mary I's two-foot Page of Honour, John Jarvis.
6. In Saudi Arabia.

21

1. What talent does the Queen have that the public never sees?
2. Why was Charles voted 'hooligan of the year' by the RSPCA in 1978?
3. Which jockey was riding the Queen Mother's horse that collapsed fifty yards from the winning post in the 1956 Grand National?
4. What did Charles reply when asked if he wanted a large family immediately after William's birth?
5. Which unmarried lady-in-waiting did Queen Victoria falsely accuse of being pregnant?
6. Where did a romantic school teacher lay down his jacket for the Queen to walk on?

96

1. How did the Queen get used to the weight of the Coronation crown?
2. Why was a system called 'The Blower' installed in Clarence House?
3. How long does the Queen spend reading state papers?
4. What do the wedding rings of the ladies of the Queen's family have in common?
5. Which monarch was said to have produced twenty-one illegitimate children?
6. What people poetically call the Queen, 'the Rare White Bird of the Single Flight'?

171

1. Name the three tartans the Queen is entitled to wear.
2. Which royal was a guest on Maria Aitken's television chat show?
3. Who writes Prince Charles's speeches?
4. What's the significance of the myrtle carried in all royal bridal bouquets?
5. Who was the first truly British Queen Consort for 450 years?
6. On which tour did Margaret cause an uproar by calling the Irish 'pigs'?

21

1. She's a superb mimic and specializes in taking off politicians.
2. He went on a boar hunt in Liechtenstein.
3. Dick Francis.
4. 'Bloody hell, give us a chance.'
5. Lady Flora Hastings.
6. In Jamaica in 1953.

96

1. She wore it round the Palace for a few days before the ceremony.
2. To ensure that the Queen Mother can always follow horse racing.
3. Two or three hours a day.
4. They are all made from the same lump of Welsh gold.
5. Henry I.
6. The Maoris.

171

1. The Royal Stewart, the Hunting Stewart and the Balmoral Tartan.
2. Princess Michael.
3. He writes them himself.
4. It's picked from a bush grown from the myrtle that was in Queen Victoria's wedding bouquet.
5. The Queen Mother.
6. On her 1977 tour of America.

22

1. What crossword puzzle does the Queen try to make time for every day?
2. Which member of the Royal Family is famous for her 'blistering tongue'?
3. What send-off did Charles's shipmates give him when he left the Navy?
4. What things old, borrowed and blue did Diana wear on her wedding day?
5. Who said, 'Mother dear is the most selfish person I have known'?
6. Where did the Queen write her cues for New Zealand's State Opening of Parliament?

97

1. What is the Queen's star sign?
2. Which member of the Royal Family had his school exercise book stolen and offered for sale?
3. When did Andrew get his Navy promotion from sub-lieutenant to full lieutenant?
4. How many times were Charles and Diana photographed together during their courtship?
5. Name two monarchs who died on the loo?
6. What unusual gift was presented to the Queen in Gambia for Prince Andrew?

172

1. Which lake did the Queen fall into looking for ducks' eggs as a child?
2. Which great musician played at Charles's twenty-first birthday party?
3. What setting was chosen for the Queen's first televized Christmas broadcast?
4. What brought Margaret's romance with Roddy to an end?
5. What notice hung in George VI's bathroom in Buckingham Palace?
6. How did Prince Philip's mother earn money during the family's exile in Paris?

22

1. The *Telegraph*'s.
2. Princess Anne.
3. They pushed him ashore in a wheel chair with a lavatory seat and garlands of toilet paper round his neck.
4. The lace panels on her dress were old, the tiara borrowed and the bow on her waistband blue.
5. George V, about Queen Alexandra.
6. On her white glove.

97

1. Taurus.
2. Prince Charles.
3. In 1984.
4. Never.
5. George II and Catherine the Great.
6. A two-year-old crocodile in a pierced silver biscuit box.

172

1. The lake at Buckingham Palace.
2. Yehudi Menuhin.
3. The long library, once the bowling alley, at Sandringham.
4. He fell in love with Tania Soskin.
5. 'Cleanliness is next to godliness'.
6. She ran a shop selling Greek embroidery and works of art.

23

1. Who is the Queen's corsetiere?
2. What does Charles do with the million or so oysters produced each year from his oyster beds in Cornwall?
3. How many rooms are there in Buckingham Palace?
4. To whom did Princess Margaret become unofficially engaged after her affair with Townsend?
5. Who was the first person to pay homage to Elizabeth as Queen?
6. Where was Prince Philip when he said, 'I declare this thing open – whatever it is'?

98

1. When did the US vote the Queen the 'Third Most Admired Woman in the World' with Eleanor Roosevelt and Jackie Kennedy?
2. Who said, 'I'm delighted I didn't have a sister'?
3. What was the title of Prince Philip's collected writings published in 1984?
4. How long after they met did Margaret take Roddy to Mustique?
5. What did George V say on appointing Britain's first Labour prime minister?
6. Where did Charles take Diana's sister, Sarah, for a skiing holiday in February 1978?

173

1. How tall is the Queen?
2. What does Prince Philip's passport list as his occupation?
3. How many hours of embroidery went into the Queen's Coronation dress?
4. What did Anne buy in a Knightsbridge shop shortly before her wedding?
5. How did the Royal Family refer to George VI's famous rages?
6. Who was the first member of the Royal Family to fly around the world?

23

1. Mrs Tess Seidan.
2. He sub-contracts the marketing rights to MacFisheries Ltd.
3. Over 600.
4. Billy Wallace.
5. Her grandmother, Queen Mary.
6. Vancouver, 1969.

98

1. 1961.
2. Princess Anne.
3. 'Men, Machines and Sacred Cows'.
4. Six months.
5. 'I wonder what Grandmama [Queen Victoria] would have thought.'
6. Klosters, Switzerland.

173

1. 5 foot 4 inches.
2. Prince of the Royal House.
3. 3000 hours.
4. A Victorian-style white broderie anglaise négligé and four white nightgowns.
5. His 'gnashes'.
6. The Queen Mother.

24

1. What cameras does the Queen use to take her own snaps?
2. Where and how did Prince Philip narrowly escape death?
3. At what age did Charles start receiving the revenues of the Duchy of Cornwall?
4. Why was Jeremy Fry vetoed as Snowdon's best man?
5. How did the Duke of Windsor describe his outfit for his Investiture as Prince of Wales?
6. Who wrote to George VI, 'As one father to another, we can be proud of our daughters'?

99

1. Name the two major criticisms of the Queen's entourage?
2. How old was Princess Anne when she started at Benenden?
3. Who galvanized the BMA into investigating alternative medicine?
4. What was the age gap between Margaret and Townsend?
5. Who got punished when Edward VI did badly at his lessons?
6. Who called Margaret 'one hip chick'?

174

1. What was the weather like on the Queen's Coronation day?
2. How much does Charles spend each year on his team of polo ponies?
3. How many people watched the first showing of the *Royal Family* TV film in 1969?
4. Who said, 'Being pregnant is an occupational hazard of being a wife'?
5. For which monarch was the Imperial State Crown made?
6. Where did fifteen-year-old Prince Philip vomit into his top hat?

24

1. A Rollei or a Leica.
2. At Cowes. A crane crashed to the ground, missing him by inches.
3. On his twenty-first birthday.
4. Because of a homosexual conviction in 1952.
5. A 'preposterous rig'.
6. President Truman.

99

1. No top blacks and no top women.
2. Thirteen.
3. Prince Charles.
4. He was sixteen years her senior.
5. His whipping boy, Barnaby Fitzpatrick.
6. Louis Armstrong.

174

1. It drizzled.
2. Around £40,000.
3. Twenty-three million.
4. Princess Anne.
5. Queen Victoria.
6. Athens, which he was visiting for the first time since infancy.

25

1. What is the total value of the Queen's jewels?
2. Which royal describes herself as having 'tiny boobs and big shoulders'?
3. When was Prince Philip created Duke of Edinburgh?
4. Which of Charles's girlfriends worked in an orphanage in war-torn Saigon?
5. Who shared George V's breakfast table?
6. What did the Queen Mother reply when asked, on her 1938–9 Canadian tour, if she was Scottish or English?

100

1. Who told the Queen she looked like 'an orchid in cellophane'?
2. Who declared an 'inherited inability to keep his mouth shut'?
3. Why did Buckingham Palace footmen stop powdering their hair in 1969?
4. Where and when did Prince George propose to Princess Marina?
5. Why was the Queen Mother short on Royal Jewels when Queen Consort?
6. Why did the Queen have to change in mid-procession from her Landau to a jeep during her 1984 Canadian Tour?

175

1. How did the Vice-Provost of Eton address the Queen and her sister when he gave them lessons as children?
2. What is the Queen Mother's family name?
3. What royal London landmark was voted by a 1986 survey as the most disappointing to tourists?
4. Who piloted the honeymoon plane taking Charles and Diana to Gibraltar?
5. How did fat Henry VIII get on his horse?
6. Who was addressed as 'His Most Christian Majesty'?

25

1. Their value is incalculable.
2. Princess Michael.
3. On his wedding day.
4. Davina Sheffield.
5. His pet parrot, Charlotte.
6. 'Since we've been in Quebec, I've been Canadian.'

100

1. Prince Philip's equerry, on seeing her riding for the first time in a glass-roofed Cadillac in Canada.
2. Prince Charles.
3. Prince Philip thought it wasn't manly.
4. In a log cabin in Yugoslavia in August 1934.
5. Queen Mary hung on to them all until she died, when they passed to the Queen.
6. One of the horses drawing the landau reared up in fright at the twenty-one-gun salute.

175

1. 'Gentlemen'.
2. Strathmore.
3. Buckingham Palace.
4. Prince Charles.
5. Pulleys hoisted him into the saddle.
6. The King of France.

26

1. How many carriages and how many cars does the Queen maintain?
2. Who said, 'My children are not royal; they just happen to have the Queen for their aunt'?
3. Which royal is president of the Football Association and the All England Lawn Tennis and Croquet Club?
4. What room at the Palace is traditionally used for royal christenings?
5. What action did George III take after discovering a louse on his dinner plate?
6. Which German school did Prince Philip attend after Cheam?

101

1. Where and when did the Queen make her last curtsey?
2. Which royal described a Henry Moore sculpture as looking like 'a monkey's gallstone'?
3. How are the carpets in the Palace State Apartments cleaned?
4. What did Colin Tennant give Margaret as a wedding present?
5. Which vain old Queen refused to have any mirrors in her rooms?
6. Where did Philip make the Queen smile with the message, 'Remember the wailing and gnashing of teeth'?

176

1. How often do the women-of-the-bedchamber enter the Queen's bedroom?
2. Which male members of the Royal Family wear contact lenses?
3. Which suite is given to Buckingham Palace's most prestigious guests?
4. How long was Diana in labour with William?
5. In whose opinion is George III a 'much maligned man and monarch'?
6. Where did Prince Philip go dancing with the price tag still attached to his jeans?

26

1. Seventy carriages and about twenty cars.
2. Princess Margaret.
3. The Duke of Kent.
4. The Music Room.
5. He ordered all his kitchen staff to shave their heads.
6. Salem.

101

1. To her father's body in St George's Chapel, Windsor.
2. Prince Philip.
3. They are brushed with velvet padded brooms.
4. A ten-acre plot on Mustique.
5. Elizabeth I.
6. In Canada, before her first television broadcast.

176

1. Never.
2. Mark Phillips and Prince Philip.
3. The Belgium Suite.
4. Sixteen hours.
5. Prince Charles.
6. During the 1951 tour of Canada.

27

1. What famous comment did the Queen make when sending small Prince Charles to find a lost dog lead?
2. Who taught Prince Philip to paint?
3. Where are Buckingham Palace's staff bedrooms located?
4. Who shared the Queen Mother's nine-foot-high wedding cake?
5. Which wife did Henry VIII call 'the Flander's Mare' and 'the Dutch Cow'?
6. Where was the Queen's jewel case mistakenly loaded onto a normal commercial flight?

102

1. Which of the Queen's fashion accessories have most often been called dowdy?
2. How many O-levels did Diana gain?
3. How were the stands along the Coronation route tested for safety?
4. What did the 200 non-royal guests invited to the Queen and Prince Philip's silver wedding ceremony at Westminster Abbey have in common?
5. Who was the first British monarch to own the Koh-i-Noor diamond?
6. When and where did Prince Andrew make a 280-mile canoe trip?

177

1. When the Queen was a child how did she explain the Abdication to Margaret?
2. What is the Royal Family's nickname for Princess Michael?
3. Of how many charities and organizations is the Queen Mother patron?
4. Who designed Princess Anne's wedding dress?
5. In which year did Prince Albert acquire the lease of Balmoral Castle?
6. How did Noël Coward describe the diminutive Sultan driving in the Coronation procession with the Queen of Tonga?

27

1. 'Dog leads cost money.'
2. Edward Seago.
3. On the attic floor of the east wing.
4. 100,000 underprivileged children around Britain.
5. Anne of Cleves.
6. New Zealand.

102

1. Her handbags.
2. None.
3. 500 big and heavy guardsmen stood on each one.
4. They were also celebrating their silver wedding anniversary.
5. Queen Victoria.
6. July 1977, Canada.

177

1. 'I think Uncle David wants to marry Mrs Baldwin, and Mr Baldwin doesn't like it.'
2. 'Our Val'.
3. 300.
4. Maureen Baker of Susan Small.
5. 1848.
6. As 'her lunch'.

28

1. How does the Queen like her tea?
2. Which of the Queen Mother's ladies-in-waiting is Diana's grandmother and a close friend?
3. What odd things washed up on the Cornish coast belong by right to Charles, as Duke of Cornwall?
4. How many times was Wallis Simpson divorced?
5. In what condition did the Peers leave their stalls after the Queen's Coronation?
6. Who was Prince Philip's grandfather?

103

1. Which prime minister is said to have been the Queen's favourite?
2. Name the imaginary companion invented by Princess Margaret as a child?
3. What cost-cutting measure was introduced to the Palace stables in 1983?
4. Describe the Queen's engagement ring?
5. Why was Queen Anne carried throughout her Coronation ceremony on a chair?
6. What unusual gift was presented to the Queen on her State Visit to France?

178

1. Where did the Queen buy a shilling ticket and tour a stately home unrecognized?
2. Where has Prince Philip often lost a contact lens?
3. How did Frederick Ashton honour the Queen Mother's eightieth birthday?
4. Where did Charles propose to Diana?
5. Why did Elizabeth I's Bishop of London have a tooth extracted in front of her?
6. Which son of George V was Governor General of Australia between 1945 and 1947?

28

1. Luke-warm and without a single stray tealeaf.
2. Ruth, Lady Fermoy.
3. Stranded whales, porpoises and the cargo of any ship wrecked on the Cornish coast.
4. Twice.
5. Littered with sandwich wrappings, newspapers and empty miniature bottles.
6. George I of Greece.

103

1. Harold Wilson.
2. Cousin Halifax.
3. The straw bedding was replaced by shredded newspaper.
4. One large central diamond flanked by two smaller square-cut stones with flat surfaces.
5. She was too fat and gout-ridden to walk.
6. A watch measuring five-sixteenths of an inch in diameter.

178

1. Kirby Hall, Northamptonshire.
2. On the polo field.
3. He wrote the ballet *Rhapsody* for her.
4. Over a candle-lit dinner at his apartment in Buckingham Palace.
5. To encourage her Majesty to remove some of her own rotten teeth.
6. Prince Henry, Duke of Gloucester.

29

1. How much income tax, surtax and capital gains tax does the Queen pay?
2. When and where did Charles have his appendix out?
3. How many guests were crowded into the Abbey for the Coronation?
4. Which room in Buckingham Palace was converted into a delivery room for the births of Andrew and Edward?
5. Which monarch first acquired Sandringham House and for whom?
6. Name two reasons why Margaret was criticized during her 1949 holiday in Italy?

104

1. What did the Queen reply when told by Richard Crossman that his new office was in the Elephant and Castle?
2. How large is the Queen Mother's personal staff?
3. Which member of the Queen's household not only settles the bills but also looks after her stamp collection?
4. How much was the public charged to see Princess Anne's wedding presents displayed?
5. Which two historical personages stayed at the Queen Mother's childhood home, Glamis Castle?
6. Why did Diana leave her Swiss finishing school after only one term?

179

1. What shampoo does the Queen use?
2. What was the code name of the RAF programme to get Charles to supersonic level?
3. When did the Queen and her family officially take up residence in Buckingham Palace?
4. How many guests attended the Queen and Prince Philip's wedding breakfast?
5. Who was the first King to own and drive a car?
6. When was the first official royal visit to a Communist country?

29

1. None.
2. In 1962 at the Great Ormond Street Hospital for Children.
3. 7700.
4. The bathroom of the Belgium suite.
5. Queen Victoria for the future Edward VII.
6. She had an audience with the Pope and was photographed in a swimming costume.

104

1. 'Oh, what a with-it address.'
2. Forty.
3. The Keeper of the Privy Purse.
4. 25p.
5. Mary Queen of Scots and Bonnie Prince Charlie.
6. She was desperately homesick.

179

1. A specially blended egg-and-lemon shampoo.
2. Exercise Golden Eagle.
3. 5 May 1952.
4. 150.
5. Edward VII.
6. The Snowdons' one-week tour of Yugoslavia in 1970.

30

1. What are the Queen's rules about her hats?
2. Who has greater personal wealth, Prince Charles or his father?
3. What official position in the Royal Household did Peter Townsend hold when he first met Margaret?
4. How long did the Duke of Kent and Katherine Worsley have to wait before they were allowed to get engaged?
5. What memento of Prince Albert did Queen Victoria treasure after his death?
6. Where did Prince Philip's family flee after their exile from Greece?

105

1. What are said to be the Queen's favourite TV programmes?
2. What did Lord Linley say he'd give his worst enemy for Christmas?
3. Where is the accession of a new sovereign proclaimed?
4. Which of Charles's girlfriends spoke seven languages, played the piano, harp and guitar and worked for *Vogue*?
5. In what year did George V make the first royal broadcast from Sandringham?
6. Who said, 'My parents were in short street, so they had to go abroad to economize'?

180

1. Name two occasions when the Queen appealed to the press to respect her family's privacy.
2. What was Charles's near-miss on his first parachute jump?
3. In how many countries was the *Royal Family* film shown?
4. Why was Queen Victoria's wedding dress a trend-setter?
5. Which monarch's death is said to have been hastened by euthanasia?
6. Who was addressed as His Apostolic Majesty?

30

1. They must not be too large or conceal her face from the crowd.
2. Prince Charles.
3. King's Equerry.
4. Six years.
5. His 'sweet little ear' modelled in marble.
6. Paris.

105

1. *Kojak, Dad's Army, Brideshead Revisited, The Good Life.*
2. 'Dinner with Princess Michael'.
3. St James's Palace.
4. Georgia Russel.
5. 1932.
6. Queen Mary.

180

1. When Charles started at Cheam and when Diana was pregnant with William.
2. His legs got caught in the rigging lines.
3. 130.
4. She defied the traditional royal wedding colours of silver and gold to wear virginal white.
5. George V's.
6. The Holy Roman Emperor.

31

1. Who is the Queen's gynaecologist?
2. How old was Prince Andrew when he was first seen in public?
3. Who won the Badminton Three-Day Event where Princess Anne came fifth?
4. What wedding present did the Queen receive from the Kenyan people?
5. In which monarch's reign were the crown jewels declared heirlooms and not the sovereign's personal property?
6. When was the Queen's State Visit to Rome?

106

1. What superstition does the Queen have about mealtimes?
2. Prince Charles is 5 foot 10 inches. How tall is his father?
3. What is Princess Anne's son's title?
4. Where did Margaret and Tony conduct their blossoming love affair?
5. How old was the Queen when she came to the throne?
6. Where did Prince Philip celebrate his thirtieth birthday?

181

1. What did the Queen reply to the pressman who suggested that Diana avoided attention by sending a footman to buy her winegums?
2. How does the Queen Mother sign her letters to friends?
3. Who is the Queen's Lord Lieutenant of Greater London?
4. Who said of the future George VI, 'He is a man who will be made or marred by his wife'?
5. How long did Queen Victoria reign?
6. Where did the Queen preside over the first Trooping the Colour ceremony outside Britain?

31

1. George Pinker.
2. Sixteen months.
3. Mark Phillips.
4. Sagana Lodge, near Lyeri.
5. The reign of Charles I.
6. 1961.

106

1. She won't have thirteen sitting down at table.
2. 5 foot 11½ inches.
3. He is plain Master Phillips.
4. In a ground-floor warehouse in Rotherhithe.
5. Twenty-five.
6. At sea, aboard the Magpie.

181

1. 'What a pompous remark, if I may say so.'
2. 'Ever yours'.
3. Lady Phillips.
4. Lady Strathmore, his future mother-in-law.
5. 63 years 7 months.
6. In the Berlin Olympic stadium.

32

1. Who are the Queen's Bodyguard for Scotland?
2. On how many days did press stories about Prince Charles appear during the eighty-eight days of his first term at Cheam?
3. What would the consequence for Charles have been if he'd married a Roman Catholic?
4. Who have been the three most important men in Margaret's life?
5. What hobby did George VI and the Duke of Windsor share?
6. What was the Queen's remark on first seeing the Niagara Falls?

107

1. On what occasion did the Queen preside over a stall?
2. What forced Prince Philip to give up polo?
3. What colours are the Queen's dispatch boxes from Whitehall?
4. After her divorce, who did Snowdon's mother marry?
5. When Charles is crowned King, what will his wife's coronet be known as?
6. How many nights did George VI and his family spend on a train during their 1946 tour of South Africa?

182

1. What name did the Americans give to the Queen's much copied going-away hat?
2. Which royal was in a team that once won the British bobsleigh championships?
3. Who was chairman of the Silver Jubilee Trust?
4. Which of Princess Margaret's loves lived in a commune for a year?
5. When did Queen Mary make the only two speeches of her life?
6. When and where was Charles made an honorary Indian chief of the Blackfoot tribe?

32

1. The Royal Company of Archers.
2. On sixty-eight days.
3. He would have forfeited his right to the throne.
4. Group Captain Peter Townsend, Anthony Armstrong-Jones and Roddy Llewellyn.
5. Needlework.
6. 'It looks rather damp'.

107

1. At a church fête organized by her mother in Scotland in the 1950s
2. A wrist injury.
3. Red, green and black.
4. The Earl of Rosse.
5. Queen Edith's crown.
6. Thirty-six.

182

1. 'Lilibet'.
2. Prince Michael of Kent.
3. Prince Charles.
4. Roddy Llewellyn.
5. During World War I and at her Silver Jubilee.
6. In Canada in 1977.

33

1. What did the Queen wear for Charles's wedding?
2. Whom did *Private Eye* magazine call 'the two highest-paid performing dwarves in Europe'?
3. Which member of the Royal Family is president of the International Equestrian Federation?
4. Describe Princess Margaret's engagement ring.
5. Which prime minister did Queen Victoria call a 'half-mad firebrand' and a 'deluded old fanatic'?
6. How long was the Queen's home movie of her 1953–4 Commonwealth tour?

108

1. What is Hitler's recorded opinion of the Queen as a child?
2. For which newspaper did Snowdon become artistic advisor of the colour supplement?
3. What was the value of the commemorative coin minted for the Queen's Coronation?
4. What did Charles give Anne and Mark Phillips as wedding presents?
5. Why did the Dutch jeweller faint when he cut the huge Cullinan diamond for King Edward VII?
6. How many miles did the Queen travel in her 1953–4 world tour?

183

1. What is the Queen's opinion of Princess Michael?
2. What was Princess Anne's greatest personal disappointment?
3. How many people were shot during the kidnap attempt on Princess Anne in 1974?
4. Why did the Duke of Kent and Katherine Worsley have to postpone their marriage planned for 6 May 1960?
5. Which Queen summoned her husband's mistress to his death bed?
6. How many tons of luggage accompanied the Queen on her 1953–4 world tour?

33

1. A blue dress described variously as sky, aquamarine and ice-blue.
2. Princess Margaret and Snowdon.
3. Prince Philip.
4. A ruby set in gold and surrounded by diamonds in the shape of a flower.
5. Gladstone.
6. One hour.

108

1. *'Ein fabelhaftes Kind'* (a marvellous child).
2. The *Sunday Times*.
3. A five-shilling piece.
4. He gave his sister a diamond brooch and Mark Phillips a pair of leather gun cases.
5. The emotion was too much for him.
6. 2500 miles by train, 900 by car and 10,000 by plane.

183

1. 'She's more royal than the rest of us.'
2. Not being allowed to try for a place on the British equestrian team competing in the 1972 Olympics.
3. Four.
4. Princess Margaret was marrying the same year.
5. Queen Alexandra.
6. Twelve tons.

34

1. Who brings the Queen her early-morning cup of tea in bed?
2. When did Princess Anne publicly announce she was suffering from a hangover?
3. What are the essential requirements for the bride of the heir to the British throne?
4. What confetti do the Royal Family use when pelting their newly weds?
5. Which Italian artist painted the seven panels on the State Coach?
6. Who exclaimed, 'My God, the Queen is a woman!'?

109

1. On an averagely busy day how often does the Queen change her clothes?
2. On what occasion did Charles use a disguise at Cambridge?
3. Why did the Queen change her Birthday Parade from Thursday to Saturday?
4. How was the Duke of Windsor's mistress, Mrs Freda Dudley Ward, informed that their relationship was over?
5. What condition did Queen Victoria make when agreeing to a medical school being named after her?
6. What was Prince Philip's opinion of Peking?

184

1. How much taller is the Queen than her mother and sister?
2. Where does the Royal Family spend Christmas?
3. Why did the Queen ask Churchill to make his weekly call an hour later than he had for George VI?
4. Who made the Queen Mother's wedding dress?
5. Who said, 'How would you like to make a thousand speeches and never be allowed to say what you think yourself'?
6. Where did Prince Andrew spray photographers with paint?

34

1. 'Bobo' MacDonald.
2. In a speech to the Portland naval base after Charles's wedding.
3. She must be a white Anglo-Saxon Protestant.
4. Rose petals.
5. Cipriani.
6. An African chief, after meeting the Queen in Lusaka.

109

1. Three or four times.
2. To watch a student demonstration.
3. To lessen traffic congestion.
4. The switchboard operator at St James's Palace told her, 'I have orders not to put you through.'
5. That no rooms for vivisection were included in it.
6. 'A deathly bore'.

184

1. Two inches. She is 5 foot 4 inches; they are both 5 foot 2 inches.
2. Windsor Castle.
3. She wanted to continue bathing and putting her children to bed.
4. Handley Seymore.
5. The Duke of Windsor, when King.
6. In Los Angeles in 1984.

35

1. How did the eleven-year-old Queen inscribe the account she'd written for her parents of their Coronation?
2. Where does Prince Charles buy his shirts and ties?
3. Why was the Queen unable to attend the last-ever presentation of Commonwealth débutantes?
4. Where did the Queen and Prince Philip spend their honeymoon?
5. For what purpose did Henry VIII form the Yeoman of the Guard?
6. What horse did Princess Anne ride in the 1976 Olympic games in Montreal?

110

1. What do the Royal Family call the Queen when she's in a bad mood?
2. In which A-level subject did Prince Charles gain a distinction?
3. Who took the official Coronation photographs?
4. Why did Prince Michael of Kent renounce his rights of succession to the throne?
5. Where was the Duke of Windsor's last public appearance as King?
6. What politically sensitive act did the Queen carry out on her 1984 visit to Jordan?

185

1. Who of the Queen's prime ministers was said to have been her ardent admirer?
2. Which Navy Command examination paper did Philip fail?
3. Who was the last débutante to be presented to the Queen?
4. How many quill pens were used to write out the Queen Mother's ornate marriage licence?
5. How old was Queen Victoria when she came to the throne?
6. How much luggage did the Queen take on her visit to Mexico?

35

1. 'To Mummy and Pap, in memory of their Coronation from Lilibet, By Herself.'
2. Turnbull and Asser.
3. She had sinusitis.
4. First at Broadlands, then Birkhall on the Balmoral Estate.
5. For the 'protection of the dignity and grandeur of the English Crown forever'.
6. Goodwill.

110

1. 'Piggyface'.
2. His optional history paper.
3. Cecil Beaton.
4. To marry the divorced, Catholic Baroness Marie Christine von Reibnitz.
5. The British Legion Festival in the Albert Hall on Armistice Night.
6. She laid a wreath to Arab soldiers killed fighting against Israel.

185

1. Winston Churchill.
2. 'Torpedo and Asdic'.
3. Fiona MacCrae.
4. Twenty.
5. Eighteen.
6. An estimated six tons.

36

1. What jewellery does the Queen most commonly wear?
2. Which close relative of the Queen also found an intruder in her bedroom?
3. What will Prince Philip drink before an official meal?
4. Which newspaper told Margaret, 'Give up Roddy or quit'?
5. Why did the radical press dub Queen Victoria 'Mrs Brown'?
6. Where did Charles first represent the Queen abroad?

111

1. What did the Queen reply when her mother said she would live to be a hundred?
2. Which royal couple have a butler who once worked for Bing Crosby?
3. How did the chemist improve his sense of smell before preparing the anointing oil for the Queen's Coronation?
4. Name four show-biz celebrities at Andrew and Fergie's wedding?
5. What occurrences were interpreted as bad omens during George V's funeral procession?
6. How old was Prince William when he accompanied his parents on their Australian tour?

186

1. On what vehicles did the Queen learn mechanical skills in 1945?
2. What made Diana the most copied royal of modern times?
3. What do Charles's Investiture crown and one of Billy Smart's big tops have in common?
4. What was the Queen's favourite of the hymns sung at her wedding?
5. Who was the adventurer who attempted to steal the crown jewels from Charles II?
6. On what foreign tour did the Queen brave the threat of terrorist attacks?

36

1. Pearls.
2. The Queen Mother. A deserter got into her bedroom during World War II.
3. Gin and tonic, champagne or lager.
4. The *Sun*.
5. Because of her devotion to her servant, John Brown.
6. In Malta as guest of the Governor, Sir Maurice Dorman.

111

1. 'Then it'll be Charles who'll send you your centenarian telegram.'
2. Charles and Diana.
3. He gave up smoking.
4. Andrew Andrews, Michael Caine, Billy Connolly and Elton John.
5. The Imperial Crown on the coffin came apart and the Maltese Cross fell to the ground.
6. Nine months.

186

1. On a utility vehicle and a stripped 15-cwt Bedford truck.
2. Her hairstyle.
3. They were both designed by Louis Osman.
4. 'Jesu Joy of Man's Desiring'.
5. Colonel Blood.
6. On her 1984 five-day State Visit to Jordan.

37

1. How many rooms did the Queen have demolished at her Sandringham home?
2. Who said, 'I'm heir apparent to the heir presumptive'?
3. How many races have the Queen Mother's horses won?
4. What food was served at the Queen and Prince Philip's wedding breakfast?
5. Who was the first British sovereign to go down a coal mine?
6. What record did the Queen break on the 21st April 1947?

112

1. What year was the Queen confirmed?
2. Which of his measurements has Charles always refused to reveal?
3. When did the Duke of Edinburgh inaugurate his Award for Elegant Design?
4. Which member of the Royal Family said he thought the age of thirty a good age to marry?
5. Who said, 'I won't knight buggers'?
6. When was the Duke of Windsor made Governor of the Bahamas?

187

1. Name four fancy dress costumes worn by the Queen.
2. Which members of the Royal Family became Freemasons?
3. What is the Queen doing when she pricks holes in a scroll presented by the Clerk of the Privy Council?
4. At which two weddings was Princess Anne a bridesmaid in 1960?
5. Who called Buckingham Palace 'the Shop'?
6. Who was the first British monarch to set foot in South Africa?

37

1. Ninety-one.
2. Princess Margaret when a child.
3. Over 330.
4. Sole and partridge, followed by ice cream.
5. George V.
6. She became the first heir to the throne to celebrate her 21st birthday in the Commonwealth.

112

1. 1942.
2. The measurement of his inside leg.
3. 1959.
4. Prince Charles.
5. George V.
6. 29 August 1946.

187

1. Lord Bathtub, a maid, the Spanish Infanta and a beatnik.
2. George VI and Prince Philip.
3. She is indicating the nominees for the appointment of High Sheriffs.
4. Lady Pamela Mountbatten's marriage to David Hicks and Princess Margaret's to Tony Armstrong-Jones.
5. George VI.
6. George VI.

38

1. What was the Queen's one bad habit as a child?
2. Why was Diana refused entry to the Royal Box at the 1981 Ascot?
3. When did Prince Philip make his famous statement, 'Gentlemen, I think it's time we pulled our fingers out'?
4. Why did Prince Michael of Kent spend his wedding night alone?
5. Which monarch played one performance of 'Fedora' opposite Sarah Bernhardt?
6. How often was 'God Save the Queen' sung to the Queen on her 1953–4 Commonwealth tour?

113

1. For which academic subject does the Queen admit to having a blind spot?
2. Which was the only piece of 'proper' jewellery Diana brought to her royal job?
3. Who did Anne stand in for on her first solo public engagement in 1969?
4. Which of Andrew's girlfriends made a sexy film?
5. When did the Duchess of Windsor accompany her husband to Britain for a state occasion?
6. At what Australian school did Charles spend a rugged six months in 1966?

188

1. When did the Queen pass her driving test?
2. Over what *Sun* newspaper article did the Palace seek an injunction and demand damages?
3. How many investitures does the Queen hold each year?
4. Who was the first royal baby in this country to be born in a public hospital?
5. Who designed the Balmoral tartan?
6. What did Princess Alexandra do to the Australian Governor's top hat during her 1959 visit?

38

1. She bit her nails.
2. The gate keeper failed to recognize her.
3. During a speech to the Industrial Co-partnership Association in 1961.
4. Princess Michael wanted to remain pure to receive Roman Catholic communion for the last time the next day.
5. Edward VII.
6. 508 times.

113

1. Mathematics.
2. The Spencer tiara.
3. Prince Philip.
4. Koo Stark.
5. In 1966, for the unveiling of a commemorative plaque to Queen Mary.
6. Timbertop.

188

1. She has not taken one and is not required to.
2. An article entitled 'When barefoot Di buttered my toast' written by the kitchen storeman.
3. An average of fourteen.
4. The Duke of Gloucester's son, Alexander, at St Mary's Hospital in 1974.
5. Prince Albert.
6. She sat on it.

39

1. What does the Queen share with Elizabeth I other than her name?
2. What special writing paper does the Royal Family use for their personal correspondence?
3. Who said, 'Constitutionally I don't exist'?
4. What was the Canon of Windsor's curious choice of sermon to celebrate the Queen and Prince Philip's marriage?
5. What reason did George VI have for being grateful to Lionel Logue?
6. What unique privilege did Princess Anne enjoy when competing in the 1976 Montreal Olympics?

114

1. What size glove does the Queen wear?
2. How did Snowdon's arty friends refer to Kensington Palace?
3. At what age did Charles inherit the title of Duke of Cornwall?
4. Who is the first future king to be born within sound of a railway terminal?
5. Who chose the site for Windsor Castle?
6. How many overseas visits did the Queen Mother make in 1980?

189

1. How did the Queen get her childhood nickname of 'Lilibet'?
2. What serious operation did the Queen Mother undergo in 1966?
3. When did Prince Charles make his famous attack on modern architecture?
4. What did the Archbishop of Canterbury reply when Margaret told him she wouldn't be marrying Townsend?
5. How many game birds were shot annually at Sandringham during the reign of Edward VII?
6. Which was the Queen's longest-ever foreign tour?

39

1. They both came to the throne at the age of twenty-five.
2. The 'Original Turkey Mill Kent'.
3. Prince Philip.
4. 'The Mating of the Greenfly'.
5. The Australian speech therapist helped him to control his stammer.
6. She was the only female competitor not given a sex test.

114

1. Size 7.
2. K.P.
3. At three years old.
4. Prince William.
5. William I.
6. Ten.

189

1. She gave it to herself by mispronouncing Elizabeth.
2. A colostomy.
3. Hampton Court, 1984.
4. 'What a wonderful person the Holy Spirit is!'
5. 30,000.
6. The 1953–4 Commonwealth tour which lasted six months.

40

1. When did Queen Mary give the Queen her first tiara?
2. What are Philip's nicknames for his sisters Sophia and Theodora?
3. How did the Queen Mother keep Charles quiet during his mother's Coronation?
4. What precautions did Hartnell take to keep the Queen's wedding dress secret?
5. Which of Queen Victoria's grandchildren was murdered with all her family?
6. Why did the Queen's 1953–4 Commonwealth tour make history?

115

1. To whom did the Queen bark, 'Oh, come on, get a bloody move on!'?
2. Which member of the Royal Family has a phobia about eating in public?
3. What was the Queen Mother's first public engagement?
4. With whom did the Duke of Windsor have a sixteen-year-old relationship before falling in love with Wallis Simpson?
5. By what name is the Coronation crown known?
6. Which monarch said, 'I like my own country best, climate or no, and I'll stay in it!'?

190

1. What mascot is transferred to all cars the Queen travels in?
2. How did Charles once sign the register of a university film club?
3. How did the *Royal Family* TV film affect the London water system?
4. How long was the Queen unofficially engaged to Philip?
5. Who said, 'A royal mistress should curtsey first – then jump into bed'?
6. Which member of the Royal Family made a speech in Icelandic?

40

1. When she married.
2. 'Tiny' and 'Dolla'.
3. Feeding him barley sugar.
4. He whitewashed the windows of his salon and his manager slept on the premises.
5. Tsarina Alexandra.
6. It was the first time ever that a British Sovereign had circumnavigated the globe.

115

1. To the policeman who finally arrived to arrest the intruder, Fagin, in her bedroom.
2. Princess Diana.
3. An RAF pageant in Hendon in June 1923.
4. Mrs Freda Dudley Ward.
5. St Edward's Crown.
6. George V.

190

1. A silver model of St George and the Dragon.
2. 'Charlie Chester'.
3. Because viewers waited for the interval to go to the lavatory, the water system almost broke down.
4. Nine months.
5. Alice Keppel.
6. Prince Philip.

41

1. What present did the Queen receive from Queen Mary on her third birthday.
2. What was Charles's college at Cambridge and what was his room number?
3. How did the Queen Mother explain to toddler Charles the Royal Wave?
4. Where was George V falsely rumoured to have been secretly married and to whom?
5. How many high-explosive bombs fell on Windsor Park during World War II?
6. On which days does the Queen work while on tour and which days does she take off?

116

1. What was the high point of the thirty-ninth birthday party Margaret gave for the Queen?
2. When did Prince William make his first Buckingham Palace balcony appearance?
3. What time does the Queen have her weekly appointment with her prime minister?
4. Why did the Queen find herself celebrating her seventh wedding anniversary without Philip?
5. Why was George V horrified when he received Gandhi?
6. On the Queen's 1965 visit to West Germany, Willy Brandt and Chancellor Erhardt fought over the right to accompany her. Who won?

191

1. Where and on what date was the Queen born?
2. Which member of the Royal Family has a reputation for 'sampling the best and giving the least'?
3. When does the Queen exercise political authority?
4. How did Mark Phillips keep himself occupied while Anne was in labour with their first child?
5. What traditional saying is connected with the Coronation ring?
6. How many dresses did the Queen have made for her short visit to Japan?

41

1. A clockwork monkey.
2. Trinity College. His room number was six.
3. 'This is how you do it, it is like opening a huge jar of sweets.'
4. In Malta, to the daughter of Admiral Culme-Seymour.
5. 500.
6. She works Tuesday to Saturday inclusive and takes Sunday and Monday off.

116

1. The première of a home movie starring Margaret, Tony, Peter Sellers and an eight-month pregnant Britt Ekland.
2. In 1984, after Trooping the Colour.
3. At 5 p.m.
4. He was attending a dinner celebrating the Charge of the Light Brigade.
5. Because he had 'no proper clothes on and bare knees'.
6. They both accompanied her.

191

1. 17 Bruton Street, London W1, on 21 April 1926.
2. Princess Margaret.
3. When she appoints ministers and dissolves Parliament.
4. He read the *Horse and Hound*.
5. 'The closer the fit the longer the reign'.
6. Thirty.

42

1. How does the Queen drink her coffee?
2. Who told his daughter, 'Remember you are a human being first and a lady second'?
3. Who is the Supreme Governor of the Church of England?
4. When was the world press reporting a serious rift in the Queen's marriage?
5. Name the ruby which has been in every monarch's crown since Charles I?
6. How many countries did the Queen visit on her 1953–4 Commonwealth tour?

117

1. What was Queen Mary's nickname for the Queen as a child?
2. What sport did Prince Philip take up when he could no longer play polo?
3. What were the topics of the Queen's first conversation with Richard Crossman?
4. Which newspapers printed sneaked photographs of a pregnant Diana in a bikini?
5. Which monarch commissioned Fabergé to sculpt models of Sandringham's farm animals?
6. Who said, 'I've met all the kings now I've met the Queen of England'?

192

1. Listening to a hymn as a child, the Queen misheard 'all mankind' as 'old man kind'. Who she think it referred to?
2. Who interviewed Prince Charles on his first radio broadcast in 1969?
3. What error did the Queen make during her Coronation?
4. Where did Prince Philip hold his stag party?
5. Which royal lady kept the last court dwarf in England?
6. When did the Queen return the 1971 visit of Emperor Hirohito of Japan?

42

1. Milky with sugar.
2. Lord Snowdon.
3. The Queen.
4. During Philip's 1956–7 four-month Commonwealth tour.
5. The Black Prince's Ruby.
6. Twelve.

117

1. 'The bambino'.
2. Carriage driving.
3. Her corgis and cows.
4. The *Star* and the *Sun*.
5. Edward VII.
6. Mohamed Ali after meeting the Queen in America in 1976.

192

1. Her grandfather, George V.
2. Jack de Manio.
3. Supposed to remove all her jewellery when donning the white linen shift, she forgot her earrings.
4. The Belfry Club.
5. Princess Augusta, mother of George III.
6. In May 1975.

43

1. Which is the Queen's favourite room in Buckingham Palace?
2. Which woman has the Queen Mother never been able to forgive?
3. How long was Charles's stint in the Navy?
4. Where was Princess Anne conceived?
5. Before Buckingham Palace, which was the principal royal residence in London?
6. Where did Prince Philip outrageously call the Queen's Christmas Broadcast 'The Queen's Show'?

118

1. How large is the Queen's private fortune?
2. Where was the Duke of Gloucester living when he inherited his title?
3. In which year did the *Daily Express* vote Princess Anne 'Sportswoman of the Year'?
4. What was attached to Andrew and Fergie's carriage as they drove away from the Abbey after their wedding?
5. Which monarch won the RAF doubles at Wimbledon?
6. When did George V stomach his dislike of going abroad and visit British troops in North Africa?

193

1. Which is the most famous diamond in the Queen's private collection?
2. Whom did the Royal Family nickname 'Princess Pushy'?
3. What duties are the Queen's councillors of state not allowed to carry out in her absence?
4. What message does Philip send the Queen when he goes away?
5. Why did James I walk like a duck?
6. When did the Queen make a private visit to the British Army on the Rhine?

43

1. The White Drawing Room.
2. Wallis Simpson.
3. Five years.
4. Malta.
5. St James's Palace.
6. Toronto.

118

1. It is speculated to be between £50 and £100 million.
2. In a converted warehouse in the Docklands.
3. 1971.
4. A giant teddy bear and a practical-joke satellite dish.
5. George VI, with Louis Greig.
6. June 1943.

193

1. The rose-coloured diamond cut to 23.60 carats made as an Alpine rose.
2. Princess Michael.
3. Dissolve parliament, disband units of the Army or grant any rank, dignity or title.
4. 'The Lord watch between thee and me when one is absent from the other.'
5. Terrified of being stabbed, he wore layers of heavily padded clothing that impeded his movements.
6. 1984.

44

1. How much older is the Queen than Margaret?
2. What year did Philip have a 'near-miss' aircraft collision?
3. How many telephones are there in Buckingham Palace?
4. Who said of Charles and Diana's wedding, 'No Hollywood producer could possibly have matched what I saw today'?
5. What did Queen Victoria call votes for women?
6. When did Philip tell students in China, 'If you stay here much longer you'll go back with slitty eyes'?

119

1. What was the Queen wearing the moment she became Elizabeth II?
2. What is the Queen Mother's dress size?
3. Who described his royal appointment as 'not by any means beer and skittles'?
4. Who baked Princess Anne's 5 foot 8 inch-high wedding cake?
5. Why did Queen Victoria smoke?
6. What personal reason was behind Prince Philip's unscheduled dash to Munich in August 1966?

194

1. How many ladies-in-waiting does the Queen have?
2. What did Princess Michael say when she turned up for dinner with the Queen and her family forty minutes late?
3. How many guests are invited to each of the four garden parties the Queen gives a year?
4. How long was Fergie's wedding train?
5. For what pet project did James I use the site of Buckingham Palace?
6. Who was the first British monarch to visit Japan?

44

1. Four years and four months.
2. 1981.
3. Over 300, including extensions.
4. Richard Burton.
5. 'A mad, wicked folly'.
6. On the 1986 Royal Tour of China.

119

1. Brown slacks, yellow shirt and a cardigan.
2. Size fourteen.
3. The Queen's first private secretary, Sir Alan Lascelles.
4. The Army Catering Corps.
5. To keep flies away.
6. To supervise his sick mother's return to Athens.

194

1. Eight.
2. 'Please don't get up, anyone.'
3. About 9000.
4. 17 foot.
5. A silkworm factory.
6. The Queen, in 1975.

45

1. Which of the performing arts does the Queen privately find an ordeal?
2. When did Snowdon water-ski across the Channel and back in a gale?
3. How is the Queen transported to the State Opening of Parliament?
4. Where did Diana buy underwear the day before her engagement announcement?
5. Who said, 'We sailors never smile on duty'?
6. When did the Prince and Princess of Wales use the alias 'Mr and Mrs Hardy'?

120

1. Why does the Queen never wear jersey fabric?
2. Which poet was one of the Queen Mother's closest friends?
3. On which programme did Princess Anne make her TV debut?
4. How many telegrams were received by the Palace in the twenty-four hours after Andrew was born?
5. What was the Royal Family's nickname for George VI?
6. What beauty treatment did a group of Australian workmen undertake before being presented to the Queen?

195

1. In what does the Queen boil the water for her private cup of tea?
2. Which of the Queen Mother's residences does she actually own?
3. When did the Queen create Princess Anne Dame Grand Cross of the Royal Victorian Order?
4. What was the Queen's first proper married home?
5. Which Queen ordered the laying-out of the Royal Ascot race course?
6. What was Charles's quip on being confronted with twelve Diana look-alikes on a visit to New Zealand?

45

1. Opera.
2. In 1967, as one of a four-man relay team.
3. In the Irish State Coach drawn by a team of Windsor Greys.
4. The Janet Reger shop in Knightsbridge.
5. George V.
6. In 1981 flying to the Bahamas on holiday.

120

1. It's too clinging and the hems tend to drop.
2. Sir John Betjeman.
3. Blue Peter.
4. 4000.
5. 'The Foreman'.
6. They removed the callouses from their hands with sandpaper.

195

1. In a Victorian silver kettle converted to electricity by Philip.
2. The Castle of Mey.
3. On her twenty-fourth birthday.
4. The rented Windlesham Moor.
5. Queen Anne.
6. 'Not as good as the real thing.'

46

1. Who was the first woman physician to the Queen?
2. What was the aptly named hotel where fourteen-year-old Charles drank his famous cherry brandy?
3. Of how many associations is Prince Philip patron?
4. Who designed the Queen's wedding gown?
5. Which monarch asked President Truman for his autograph?
6. Why did the Queen Mother insist on being alone on long car drives during her 1960 official visit to Rhodesia and Nyasaland?

121

1. With what words does the Palace switchboard connect the Queen with her mother?
2. Who is Prince Charles's tailor?
3. How many works were exhibited at the 1977 'Royal Performance' art show at Windsor.
4. What water is traditionally used for the christening of royal babies?
5. Who made George V laugh so much after an operation that he burst his stitches?
6. What brought three-month-old Prince Philip on his first visit to England?

196

1. When did the Queen start teaching Anne to ride?
2. What supernatural gift does the Queen Mother claim to possess?
3. What was Prince Charles's first solo engagement?
4. What is Queen Victoria reputed to have said when told her childbearing days were over?
5. When and why was the office of Private Secretary to the Monarch created?
6. Who was the sex symbol presented to Princess Anne on her 1984 visit to America?

46

1. Dr Margery Blackie, a homeopathist.
2. The Crown.
3. Nearly 400.
4. Norman Hartnell.
5. George VI.
6. She wanted to take off her shoes, put her feet up and eat butterscotch.

121

1. 'Your Majesty? Her Majesty, Your Majesty.'
2. Hawes and Curtis of Dover Street.
3. Fifty works by past and present members of the Royal Family.
4. Water from the River Jordan.
5. The Rt Hon. J. (Jimmy) H. Thomas.
6. The funeral of his maternal grandfather, Prince Louis of Battenberg.

196

1. When Anne was two and a half.
2. The gift of second sight.
3. Touring the British Sugar Corporation in King's Lynn at Christmas 1958.
4. 'Oh, doctor, can I have no more fun in bed?'
5. In 1805, when George III was no longer able to see well enough to do his work.
6. Joan Collins.

47

1. What is the Queen's favourite musical instrument?
2. Why did Diana burst into tears in public in 1981?
3. When and where was Charles invested Prince of Wales?
4. How many cocoons were used to produce the sixty yards of 54-inch wide satin needed for the Queen's wedding gown?
5. Who complained of a 'defect in the Constitution' that allowed a party to come to power 'merely on account of the number of votes'?
6. On the Queen's 1965 visit to West Germany, newspapers printed instruction for 'Hofknick'. What were they?

122

1. What untrue story is told about the fate of the Queen's discarded clothes?
2. Which of his schools did Prince Charles say was 'just like prison'?
3. Who said, 'I have been trained since childhood never to show emotion in public'?
4. What line did Charles fluff at his wedding ceremony?
5. Who was the first monarch to install a loo?
6. Name the ship that brought Philip and his exiled family from Greece.

197

1. When did a youth fire five blank shots at the Queen?
2. Where does Charles get his hair cut?
3. What is the function of the Gentleman Usher of the Black Rod?
4. What did the Duchess reply when the Duke of Windsor asked, 'What would you have if you were granted one wish'?
5. Who was the first king's son to marry in Westminster Abbey for 541 years?
6. What was Anne's reply to the photographer in Amsterdam who said, 'Look this way, love'?

47

1. The bagpipes.
2. When she saw Charles's horse, Allibar, collapse and die of a massive heart attack.
3. 1 July 1969 at Caernarvon Castle.
4. 34,000.
5. Queen Victoria, outraged when a Liberal government was voted in.
6. 'Curtsies'.

122

1. That they are ripped up and destroyed.
2. Gordonstoun.
3. The Queen.
4. He promised to share all *her* goods with her!
5. Elizabeth I.
6. HMS *Calypso*.

197

1. 1981, at the Trooping the Colour ceremony.
2. Truefitt and Hill of Old Bond Street.
3. He summons the House of Commons to the Lords at the state opening of Parliament.
4. 'You'.
5. George VI.
6. 'I am not your love, I am your Royal Highness.'

48

1. How many staff look after the Queen's vast wardrobe?
2. Which magazine advises Diana on fashion?
3. At what age did the Queen Mother retire as Chancellor of London University?
4. How did Princess Margaret describe her first ten-room married home in Kensington Palace?
5. What tattoo did George V have on his right arm?
6. Where was Charles served curried snake meat?

123

1. Which of her residences does the Queen call her 'home'?
2. Name the thriller writer who sends the Queen Mother the first copy of every book of his that comes off the press?
3. What was the subject of Charles's 1974 maiden speech to the House of Lords?
4. Why were Prince Philip's sisters not invited to his wedding?
5. What did the Queen Mother reply to suggestions that her daughters should be sent to Canada for the duration of World War II?
6. How did Charles describe his six months in the Australian school, Timbertop?

198

1. How old was the Queen when she made her famous wartime broadcast on radio's *Children's Hour*?
2. Which member of the Royal Family grew up in a house with a private jester?
3. How big is Buckingham Palace's ballroom?
4. Which favourite corgi did the Queen smuggle on her honeymoon?
5. Who said 'a woman can never be too rich or too thin'?
6. Which countries did Princess Anne visit on her 1984 tour for the Save the Children Fund?

48

1. Seven.
2. *Vogue*.
3. Eighty.
4. She complained it was 'like a doll's house'.
5. A large blue and red dragon.
6. The Gurkha Survival School in Hong Kong.

123

1. Windsor Castle.
2. Dick Francis.
3. He made a plea for more government money to be spent on the nation's leisure.
4. Because they were married to Germans.
5. 'The children won't leave without me; I won't leave without the King; and the King will never leave.'
6. 'The most wonderful experience I've ever had, I think.'

198

1. Sixteen.
2. The Queen Mother.
3. 123 foot long, 60 foot wide, 45 foot high.
4. Susan.
5. The Duchess of Windsor.
6. Morocco, Gambia and Upper Volta.

49

1. How does the Queen describe Philip's appetite?
2. What is the deception connected with the Queen Mother's birth?
3. Where was Princess Anne placed in the 1971 European Three-Day Event Championship?
4. How old was the Queen when she developed a crush on Philip?
5. Which monarch first chose Buckingham Palace as her official London residence?
6. What did Edward VII have to say about Rome?

124

1. Which is the only picture ever published of the Queen in a swimming costume?
2. What was the Royal Family's nickname for Lord Mountbatten?
3. Which official is responsible for the safety of the crown jewels?
4. For which royal wedding did Cecil Beaton take the photographs?
5. What was the name of the illness that sent George III mad?
6. What was the title of the film Prince Philip made for TV on the Galápagos?

199

1. When the Queen was a child, what did she want to be when she grew up?
2. What famous comment did Prince Philip make about lavatories?
3. What is the Queen's full legal title?
4. Name the four pregnant ladies present at the 1964 New Year celebrations at Sandringham?
5. Why did Charles II's Coronation have to be postponed?
6. What did the Queen of Tonga use as her state car in Tonga?

49

1. 'Like a sparrow's.'
2. Her father put her birth place as the St Paul's Warden, Bury House, not London where she was actually born.
3. She won it.
4. Thirteen.
5. Queen Victoria.
6. 'You look at two mouldering stones and are told it's the temple of something.'

124

1. A picture taken at the Bath Club when she was thirteen.
2. Dickie.
3. The Lord Chamberlain.
4. The wedding of Princess Margaret and Tony Armstrong-Jones.
5. Porphyria.
6. *The Enchanted Isles.*

199

1. A lady living in the country with lots of dogs.
2. 'The biggest waste of water in the country by far. You spend half a pint and flush two gallons.'
3. Queen of the United Kingdom of Great Britain and Northern Ireland with its remaining Colonial Territories, and Head of the Commonwealth.
4. The Queen, Princess Alexandra, Princess Margaret and the Duchess of Kent.
5. Because Cromwell had sold all the regalia.
6. A London taxicab.

50

1. Why does the Queen never wear dark colours.
2. When did Princess Anne pass her driving test?
3. Which are the Orders over which the government has no control?
4. What did Lord Mountbatten give the Queen and Prince Philip as a wedding present?
5. What was the name of the building Sandringham House replaced?
6. Where was Princess Anne supposed to have locked Mark Phillips out of their hotel bedroom?

125

1. How much pocket money did the Queen receive as a child?
2. Which member of the Royal Family owns the Oval Cricket Ground and Dartmoor Prison?
3. Of how many regiments is the Queen Mother Colonel-in-Chief?
4. Who reputedly said of Anne and Mark Phillips, 'I shouldn't wonder if their children are four-legged'?
5. Who called Buckingham Palace a 'sepulchre'?
6. What was the Queen's comment on seeing the Sphinx in Egypt?

200

1. What was the Queen's rank in the ATS?
2. How did Prince Andrew receive a crack on the head that put him in hospital for two days?
3. How many full-time and half-time staff does Buckingham Palace employ?
4. Why was the BBC refused permission to broadcast the Queen Mother's marriage ceremony?
5. Who said, 'Presbytery is not a religion for gentlemen'?
6. Where did a dance floor collapse under the weight of the people assembled to greet Edward VII?

50

1. Because she has to stand out in a crowd.
2. April 1968.
3. The Royal Victorian Order and the Order of the Garter.
4. A cinema.
5. Sandringham Hall.
6. Hamburg, Germany.

125

1. A shilling a week.
2. Prince Charles.
3. Eighteen.
4. The Queen.
5. The Duke of Windsor.
6. 'Most disappointing'.

200

1. Second subaltern No. 230873.
2. At a dormitory fight at school.
3. 300 full-time and 120 half-time staff.
4. Because the service 'might be received by persons in public houses with their hats on'.
5. Charles I.
6. The New York Academy of Music.

51

1. What does the Queen race other than horses?
2. On what occasion did Diana wear her famous tuxedo trouser suit?
3. What great British sporting achievement was announced on the day of the Queen's Coronation?
4. What floral tribute does Philip give his wife on their wedding anniversaries?
5. How long did Queen Victoria wear mourning for Albert?
6. Where did the Queen receive the news of her father's death?

126

1. How many times did the Queen see the Beatles' film *Yellow Submarine*?
2. Who said, 'The arts world thinks of me as an uncultured, polo-playing clot'?
3. How many regiments are there in the Queen's Household Division?
4. Who designed Fergie's wedding dress?
5. Who was the youngest-ever holder of the title of Prince of Wales?
6. What was Charles's unflattering verdict of St Kilda beach in Australia?

201

1. Which of the Queen's favoured designers made the clothes for her gala occasions?
2. Who said, 'Nowadays we have to compete with Elizabeth Taylor and The Beatles'?
3. What gave Prince Charles's eighteenth birthday special significance?
4. How many times did the Queen Mother refuse George VI's marriage proposal?
5. Who did George V telephone every single morning?
6. Who were Prince Philip's parents?

51

1. Pigeons.
2. To meet the band Genesis in 1984.
3. John Hunt's mountaineering team conquered Everest.
4. A posy of white blossoms.
5. Until the end of her life.
6. On the bank of the Sagana River, Kenya.

126

1. Four.
2. Prince Philip.
3. Seven.
4. Lindka Cierach.
5. George IV. He was created Prince of Wales at birth.
6. 'Like swimming in sewage'.

201

1. Norman Hartnell.
2. Princess Alexandra.
3. The Regency Act of 1953 decreed he could reign without a regency should his mother abdicate or die.
4. Twice.
5. His sister, Princess Victoria.
6. Prince Andrew of Greece and Princess Alice of Battenberg.

52

1. What part did the Queen play in a 1940 production of *A Christmas Child* at Windsor?
2. What was Prince Charles's first car?
3. Who writes Prince Philip's speeches?
4. How long did it take for Margaret to get her 'quickie' divorce?
5. How did Queen Victoria expect her gambling wins to be paid?
6. Who designed Princess Margaret's house on Mustique?

127

1. What moments of terror did the Queen experience on the morning of 9 July 1982?
2. What cosmetic surgery did Lord Linley have when he was three?
3. When does Trooping the Colour take place?
4. Whose wedding in 1934 was the most exciting and glittering event of the decade?
5. Who was the last British sovereign to attempt to cure the 'king's evil', scrofula, by touch?
6. Which European royal has represented his country twice at the Olympic games?

202

1. Which is the Queen's least favourite animal?
2. When and in what paper was Prince Philip first interviewed?
3. When Prince Charles became heir to the throne, what two titles did he automatically receive?
4. What was Margaret's weight gain during each pregnancy?
5. What instrument did Queen Elizabeth I play?
6. What statue did Princess Anne unveil on her 1977 visit to the USA?

52

1. She played a king.
2. An MG.
3. He writes them himself.
4. 113 seconds.
5. In newly minted coins.
6. Oliver Messel, Snowdon's uncle.

127

1. She woke to find Michael Fagin in her bedroom.
2. His sticking-out ears were corrected.
3. On the Queen's official birthday.
4. The Duke of Kent's wedding to Princess Marina of Greece.
5. Queen Anne.
6. Crown Prince Harald of Norway.

202

1. The cat.
2. 1944 in the *Newcastle Journal*.
3. The Duke of Cornwall and Rothesay.
4. Two stone.
5. The virginals.
6. A statue of Queen Anne.

53

1. What are the two affectionate nicknames given to the Queen by Palace staff?
2. Which member of the Royal Family has the famous Koh-i-Nor diamond in her crown?
3. How many maids-of-honour did the Queen have at her Coronation?
4. How many people worldwide watched Charles's and Diana's wedding on TV?
5. What two pieces of valuable advice did Queen Mary give the Duke of Windsor?
6. How many foreign visits were made by Prince Charles in 1984?

128

1. Which actress made her name impersonating the Queen?
2. When and where was Prince Charles attacked by a deranged assailant?
3. When did Princess Anne admit to experiencing 'moments of terror' on a horse?
4. Whose was the first royal marriage to be celebrated in York Minster for 633 years?
5. Which personal item did George V wear for more than fifty years?
6. Which members of the Royal Family greeted Emperor Hirohito at his arrival at Gatwick Airport?

203

1. Who trains the Queen's horses?
2. Which member of the Royal Family was Diana's childhood playmate?
3. How many official engagements did the Queen carry out in 1984?
4. Why was Queen Mary outraged at the wedding present given to the Queen and Prince Philip by Gandhi?
5. After which monarch is London's King's Road named?
6. What precedent did Diana break on the Royal Tour of Australia?

53

1. 'HM' and 'Sov'.
2. The Queen Mother.
3. Six.
4. 750 million.
5. 'Never refuse an invitation to sit down, and take every opportunity to relieve yourself.'
6. Five.

128

1. Jeanette Charles.
2. In 1974 at the Royal Navy Barracks in Portland, Dorset.
3. During a BBC interview in 1974.
4. That of the Duke of Kent and Katherine Worsley.
5. A favourite gold collar stud.
6. Princess Margaret and Lord Snowdon.

203

1. Major Dick Hern.
2. Prince Andrew.
3. Over 100.
4. She mistook the crocheted tray-cloth for a loin-cloth.
5. Charles II.
6. She took her infant son, William, with her and flew with him and Charles on the same plane.

54

1. When was the communiqué 'The Queen is angry at what she considers is an intrusion of her privacy' issued?
2. Which member of the Royal Family had a footman who later changed his sex?
3. When did Charles and Anne first attend a State Opening of Parliament?
4. On what grounds did the Vatican annul Princess Michael's first marriage to Tom Troubridge?
5. How did George VI spend the last day of his life?
6. Where did thirteen-year-old Princess Anne reputedly exclaim to the Queen, 'I can't see in this bloody wind'?

129

1. Which branch of the Women's Institute does the Queen belong to?
2. What operation did the Queen Mother undergo ten days before Charles's wedding?
3. Which famous Italian artist has painted portraits of the Queen and the Queen Mother?
4. Where did the Duke of Kent meet Katherine Worsley?
5. Why did Queen Mary introduce napkin rings during World War I?
6. On what foreign visit did the Queen wear, for the first time, clothes in shades of purple, emerald and shocking pink?

204

1. What old-fashioned aircraft make up the Queen's private fleet?
2. Where did Charles write about a singing dustman and the clang of dustbins disturbing his sleep?
3. Who did Princess Anne's hair for her official twenty-first birthday photographs?
4. How much did Diana's engagement ring cost?
5. Nell Gwynne was the mistress of which monarch?
6. How many hands did the Queen shake during her Silver Jubilee Tour?

54

1. During a press siege at Sandringham by reporters anticipating the announcement of Charles's engagement to Diana.
2. Princess Margaret.
3. 31 October 1967.
4. On the grounds that he'd refused to give her children.
5. Shooting at Sandringham.
6. At a Sydney showground.

129

1. Sandringham.
2. The removal of a fish bone from her throat.
3. Pietro Annigoni.
4. Catterick Camp, Yorkshire.
5. To save on laundry costs.
6. In Rio.

204

1. Propeller-driven Andovers.
2. In an article to the Cambridge undergraduate magazine *Varsity*.
3. Michael of Michael John.
4. More than £30,000.
5. Charles II.
6. More than 5000.

55

1. Where was the Queen concealed during the TV interview given by Charles and Diana on their engagement day?
2. Which of the Queen's sons most takes after his father?
3. Which politician fell asleep in the chair next to the Queen during a Royal Air Force review?
4. Where did Princess Marina wear her wedding ring?
5. What was Henry VIII's comment on being told his wife Catherine of Aragon was dead?
6. Name the first and second husbands of Prince Philip's sister, Princess Sophie?

130

1. How did the four-year-old Queen give Margaret her nickname?
2. Which of Snowdon's photographic books is now a collector's piece?
3. What brief did the Queen give Hartnell for her Coronation dress?
4. Who said of the Queen Mother, 'She's the most marvellous person in my eyes'?
5. Who is said to haunt the library at Windsor Castle?
6. Who wrote that 'blue blood is just as red as anybody else's, the tears just as bitter'?

205

1. On what day of the week was the Queen born?
2. Who was the first royal princess to go to school?
3. Who described Buckingham Palace as 'the Museum', 'our tied cottage' and said, 'We live over the shop'?
4. Who was the youngest page at Fergie's wedding?
5. Why was George V's death reputedly hastened by euthanasia?
6. Which is the only European monarchy not to have close blood ties with the British Royal Family?

55

1. Behind a curtain.
2. Prince Andrew.
3. The then Labour Defence Minister, Fred Mulley.
4. On her right hand in accordance with Greek custom.
5. 'God be praised, the old harridan is dead!'
6. Prince Christopher of Hesse and Prince George of Hanover.

130

1. She said, 'I shall call her bud – you see, she isn't really a rose yet.'
2. *Private View*.
3. That it should be on the same lines as her wedding dress and of white satin.
4. Her husband, George VI.
5. Elizabeth I.
6. Philip's uncle, Prince Nicholas.

205

1. Wednesday.
2. Princess Alexandra.
3. Prince Philip.
4. Prince William.
5. So that the bulletin would catch the morning, rather than the evening, papers.
6. The Royal Family of the Netherlands.

56

1. Of whom did the Queen once say, 'The rapport between us is almost telepathic'?
2. Who complained that she wasn't 'supposed to appreciate anything that doesn't have four legs, barks or neighs'?
3. Which members of the Royal Family are not allowed to vote?
4. Who was the first royal bride to omit the word 'obey' in her marriage vows?
5. When was the ancient custom requiring the presence of the Home Secretary at each royal birth discontinued?
6. Which modern European monarch was a highly respected archeologist?

131

1. How does the Queen indicate that a conversation has come to an end?
2. Who said, 'If you said "Afghanistan" to Diana, she'd think it was a cheese'?
3. Why was Princess Anne barred from her mother's Coronation?
4. What was the rumoured reason for sixteen-year-old Clio Nathaniels's running away from Gordonstoun?
5. Why did bullies stick pins in fourteen-year-old George VI at Osborne Naval College?
6. Which reigning European monarch did few people expect to see crowned King?

206

1. What are the Queen's feelings about presentation bouquets?
2. Who taught Charles to fish?
3. Who was the first member of the Royal Family to make a TV broadcast?
4. Who designed Diana's wedding dress?
5. Which member of the Royal Family said, 'We are not a family, we are a firm'?
6. On what foreign visit was the Queen greeted by boos and banners telling her to 'go home'?

56

1. Her childhood nurse and friend, 'Bobo' MacDonald.
2. Princess Anne.
3. The Queen and the royal Dukes.
4. Princess Diana.
5. For Prince Charles's birth.
6. Gustavus VI of Sweden.

131

1. She smiles and takes a slight step backwards.
2. Her stepmother, Raine Spencer.
3. She was considered too young to sit still and keep quiet.
4. She'd had a lover's tiff with Prince Andrew.
5. To see if his blood was blue.
6. King Juan Carlos of Spain.

206

1. She prefers them small, not wired and using flowers in season.
2. The Queen Mother.
3. Prince Philip.
4. David and Elizabeth Emanuel.
5. George VI.
6. In Quebec, 1964.

57

1. When did the Queen say she wanted to get rid of 'all those grey-beards in satin breeches'?
2. How did Prince Charles qualify for the exclusive Ten Ton Club?
3. How many locations were used in the making of the 1969 *Royal Family* TV film?
4. At what moment did Fergie falter during her marriage ceremony?
5. What religious order was founded by Prince Philip's mother?
6. When did Prince Charles meet Mother Teresa?

132

1. What does the Queen take deer-stalking instead of a gun?
2. Which member of the Royal Family had a pony called 'Mr Dinkum'?
3. When did Prince Philip become a British subject?
4. On what date did Margaret publicly announce her decision not to marry Townsend?
5. Why did George V give up alcohol and ban its consumption in the royal household?
6. When did the Queen Mother first travel by air?

207

1. How was the Queen's favourite horse successfully cured of nervousness?
2. Who were the leaders of the famous 'Margaret Set'?
3. What was the first ship Prince Charles commanded?
4. What was the date of Andrew and Fergie's wedding?
5. Who is said to haunt the cloisters at Windsor Castle?
6. What gifts did Charles and Diana receive on their 1986 tour of Japan?

57

1. On coming to the throne.
2. He piloted a plane in excess of 1000 m.p.h.
3. 150.
4. She stumbled over Prince Andrew's middle name, Christian.
5. The Christian Sisterhood of Martha and Mary.
6. During his 1980 tour of India.

132

1. A camera.
2. Prince Andrew.
3. 28 February 1947.
4. 31 October 1955.
5. Because Lloyd George was worried about the nation's alcohol consumption and wanted the King to set an example.
6. 1 July 1935, to Brussels.

207

1. By a treatment known as 'the laying on of hands', executed by a neurologist.
2. The Earl of Dalkeith and the Marquess of Blandford.
3. The HMS *Bronington*.
4. 23 July 1986.
5. Henry VIII.
6. A car, a motorbike, two kimonos worth £40,000, a handbag and armfuls of toys.

58

1. What did the Queen give Philip on his fortieth birthday?
2. What were the names of the two pet pigs kept by the Queen Mother as a child?
3. How much money did the 1977 Silver Jubilee Appeal chaired by Prince Charles raise?
4. What other royal occasion was celebrated on Princess Anne's wedding day?
5. What did George V rank as the arch evil in the era after World War I?
6. Which foreign prime minister tried to avoid a palace reception and was sent for by the Queen?

133

1. When and from whom did the Queen get her first thoroughbred?
2. When did George VI weep through a nativity play?
3. What connection did the Queen Mother have with Virginia Woolf, Vera Brittain and Rebecca West in 1933?
4. Which royal said, 'When the fourth child comes along it's mostly unintended'?
5. Who was the first King to wear a kilt?
6. Where did the Queen spend her twenty-fourth birthday?

208

1. What special personal item does the Queen always take on her foreign trips?
2. Who said, 'I cannot imagine anything more wonderful than being who I am'?
3. Who is the Queen Mother's private secretary?
4. Why did Katherine Worsley spend a year working in a jewellers in Canada?
5. What caused George V to utter an unscripted 'God bless my soul!' when about to give his first Christmas broadcast?
6. When did the Queen go on her first walk-about?

58

1. An Alvis car.
2. Satan and Emma.
3. Sixteen million pounds.
4. Prince Charles's twenty-fifth birthday.
5. Bolshevism.
6. Ian Smith.

133

1. In 1971 as a wedding present from the Aga Khan.
2. In December 1940, overcome with emotion at watching his two daughters play the leading roles.
3. She became patron of the Careers for Women National Advisory Centre, which they pioneered.
4. Prince Philip.
5. George IV.
6. With Prince Philip in Malta.

208

1. A white kid lavatory seat.
2. Princess Margaret when a girl.
3. Sir Martin Gilliat.
4. Princess Marina thought the twenty-two-year-old Duke of Kent too young to marry and wanted them to have a separation.
5. The seat of the chair he was sitting on fell through and he found himself on the floor.
6. On the 1970 tour of New Zealand.

59

1. Why did the Queen look 'blackly furious' when a councillor, crawling backwards across the room, knocked a book off a table?
2. What was Philip's surname before his British nationalization?
3. Which parts of Buckingham Palace are open to the public?
4. What sport did Margaret take up to regain her figure after her pregnancies?
5. Which of Henry VIII's wives had hair almost down to her feet?
6. Who sent the Queen Mother a Valentine card during her 1959 tour of Kenya?

134

1. After her marriage, what compliment did Diana pay the Queen?
2. When did Princess Anne attend her first Girl Guide camp?
3. Which royal sparked off a row by criticizing modern architecture?
4. What is the sentimental association attached to the Queen's engagement ring?
5. How many meals were prepared by the Buckingham Palace kitchens during the week of George VI's Coronation?
6. Where did the Queen have her only experience of getting her hair done in a salon?

209

1. What are the Queen's racing colours?
2. What did Charles do when he had to shave off his beard?
3. How long is the robe of State worn by the Queen for the State Opening of Parliament?
4. When did Princess Alexandra and the Hon. Angus Ogilvy announce their engagement?
5. To what use was the Queen Mother's childhood home, Glamis Castle, put during World War I?
6. Which King fled from his country to Britain, where he bought the *Kensington and Chelsea Post*?

59

1. She was trying not to laugh.
2. Schleswig-Holstein-Sonderburg-Glucksberg.
3. The Royal Mews and the Queen's Gallery.
4. Water-skiing.
5. Catherine of Aragon.
6. The crew of a royal train.

134

1. She said, 'I have the best mother-in-law in the world.'
2. June 1962.
3. Prince Charles.
4. It was redesigned from Prince Philip's mother's engagement ring.
5. 18,832.
6. In Malta in 1949.

209

1. Red and blue.
2. He collected the shavings into matchboxes and sent them to those in his family who'd been most critical of the beard.
3. 18 ft.
4. 29 November 1962.
5. It was a hospital for 1500 wounded soldiers.
6. King Zog of Albania.

60

1. How does Philip describe the Queen's worrying?
2. Who is the Queen Mother's favourite author?
3. Why was Diana horrified at the widely published photograph taken of her in the garden of her nursery school?
4. Which was the first royal wedding to be televized live?
5. Which queen bought a large selection of the Imperial Russian jewels when they came on the market after the Revolution?
6. How many tours and how many countries did the Queen visit in 1983?

135

1. Which of her horses made the Queen the 1954 leading British owner in terms of stake money?
2. What part did Prince Edward play in Gordonstoun's production of *Black Comedy* by Peter Shaffer?
3. Who described the young Queen as discharging her duties 'as near to perfection as a mortal can'?
4. What did Barbara Cartland wear to watch her step-granddaughter marry Prince Charles on TV?
5. When was the Instrument of Abdication signed?
6. Who should be addressed as His Most Catholic Majesty?

210

1. What did the Queen and her sister call George V when they were children?
2. Who joked, 'The chopper changed my life as conclusively as that of Anne Boleyn'?
3. Who advises the Queen on situations affecting Crown, country and Commonwealth?
4. How much was Philip earning as a lieutenant when he married the Queen?
5. What was the date of Charles I's execution?
6. Where were Mark Phillips and other members of the British equestrian team accused of acting like 'upper-class hooligans'?

60

1. Her 'fretwork'.
2. P. G. Wodehouse.
3. Her skirt was transparent and the whole length of her legs was visible.
4. Princess Margaret's wedding to Tony Armstrong-Jones.
5. Queen Mary.
6. She made fifty tours and visited 100 countries.

135

1. Aureole.
2. The male lead.
3. Lord Chandos, then Colonial Secretary.
4. The uniform of the St John Ambulance Brigade, of which she is chairperson.
5. 10 December 1936.
6. The King of Spain.

210

1. Grandpapa England.
2. The Queen Mother.
3. Her private secretary.
4. 26 shillings a day, plus 18s 6d a day married allowance.
5. 30 January 1649.
6. On the ferry crossing from Holland to Harwich in June 1981.

61

1. How many children formed the Queen's Buckingham Palace Girl Guide pack?
2. Who was the first member of the Royal Family to be murdered since the seventeenth century?
3. What was the total 1980 income of the Duchy of Cornwall.
4. Which of his newly born sons did Prince Philip say reminded him of a 'plum pudding'?
5. How many Orders of the British Empire were bestowed between 1917–22?
6. Where did Prince Edward get his first taste of official life?

136

1. What did the chambermaid exclaim when she saw the intruder, Fagin, sitting on the Queen's bed?
2. Diana weighed over ten stone when she first met Charles. How much did she weigh in 1986?
3. What word is never used when addressing royalty?
4. What romantic rumour about the Queen Mother circulated in American newspapers in the 1950s?
5. Prince Charles is the twenty-fourth Duke of Cornwall. Who was the first?
6. What did the Queen diplomatically wear when formally welcomed to China?

211

1. What did the Queen wear for her father's Coronation?
2. Who sold pictures of Princess Margaret impersonating Sophie Tucker to a national newspaper?
3. Who is the Duke of Lancaster?
4. What was Princess Anne's reason for having only two small attendants at her wedding?
5. Which monarch had three Derby wins and won the Grand National?
6. When did Philip first take the Queen to his homeland, Greece?

61

1. Thirty-four.
2. Earl Mountbatten of Burma.
3. £32 million.
4. Prince Charles.
5. 25,000.
6. Canada. In 1978 he planted a commemorative tree at Lloydminster.

136

1. 'Bloody hell, Ma'am, what's he doing here?'
2. Eight stone.
3. 'You'.
4. That she was planning to marry her treasurer, Sir Arthur Penn.
5. The Black Prince.
6. A red outfit to match the red Communist flags that filled Peking's huge square.

211

1. A long silver dress, pearls and a purple cloak lined with ermine.
2. Colin Tennant's heroin-addicted son.
3. The Queen!
4. She didn't want 'hordes of uncontrollable children' around.
5. Edward VII.
6. 1950.

62

1. Which prime minister was persuaded by the Queen and her sister when children, to slide down a slope on a tea-tray?
2. Who called university 'a very much over-rated pastime'?
3. How many gems are there in the Imperial State Crown?
4. What was served at Andrew and Fergie's wedding breakfast?
5. How large was Elizabeth I's wardrobe?
6. How many hands did the Queen shake during a reception in Washington in 1976?

137

1. How large was the Queen's and her sister's childhood collection of dolls?
2. What did Princess Margaret call her 'Papa's dress'?
3. Why did the Queen Mother once refuse tea at a Women's Institute meeting?
4. When and where did the Prince and Princess Michael of Kent get married?
5. How was Queen Victoria trained as a child to hold her head up when eating?
6. Which monarchy claims to be the oldest dynasty in Europe?

212

1. Why doesn't the Queen have to obey the laws of the land?
2. Who said, 'The man who invented the red carpet ought to have his head examined'?
3. When was Harold Wilson caught out unprepared by the Queen?
4. Who was the page who fell over carrying the Queen's train at her wedding?
5. Which monarch is Hanover Square named for?
6. In which Olympics did Princess Anne compete as a member of the British equestrian team?

62

1. Neville Chamberlain.
2. Princess Anne.
3. 3250.
4. Lobster and lamb.
5. It contained over 200 dresses.
6. 1574.

137

1. They had 150.
2. Her first evening dress that was a favourite of George VI.
3. She'd spied something she preferred – sherry!
4. 30 July 1978 in the Vienna town hall.
5. A sprig of holly was tied under her chin.
6. The Danish monarchy.

212

1. Because they are *her* laws, and the courts are *her* courts.
2. Prince Philip.
3. In 1964. He hadn't read the proposal for Milton Keynes that she wanted to discuss.
4. Prince Michael of Kent.
5. George I.
6. The 1976 Olympic games in Montreal.

63

1. Where does the Queen spend her summer holidays?
2. Why do the Royal Family stay on the *Britannia* when visiting the Queen Mother at the Castle of Mey?
3. Which are the two favourite annual engagements on the royal calender?
4. How many wedding presents did Princess Anne and Mark Phillips receive?
5. Who said, 'An ugly baby is a very nasty object – and the prettiest is frightful'?
6. What were Princess Margaret's departing words to the Governor of Kenya in the 1950s?

138

1. When a guest, the Queen once had to watch her horse racing on a TV in a butler's sitting room. Why?
2. Which member of the Royal Family plays the piano, the trumpet and the cello?
3. Which Order founded in 1902 is the monarch's own gift?
4. Where did the Duke of Windsor and Wallis Simpson marry?
5. What was the first recorded building on the site of St James's Palace?
6. What distance did the Queen cover between 1952–7 on foreign tours?

213

1. What was special about the lipstick the Queen wore for her Coronation?
2. With what three definitions does Princess Michael reputedly describe herself, Diana and Sarah?
3. What is the motto of the Prince of Wales?
4. How long did Diana stay in hospital for the birth of her second son?
5. Which monarch insisted that clocks at Sandringham were kept half an hour early?
6. In what country is the Queen known as 'the English Female King'?

63

1. Balmoral.
2. The Castle of Mey isn't large enough to accommodate them all.
3. The Chelsea Flower Show and Royal Ascot.
4. Over 2000.
5. Queen Victoria.
6. 'See you later, alligator!'

138

1. Because her hosts didn't keep a TV in the big house.
2. Prince Charles.
3. The Order of Merit.
4. At the Château de Cande, France.
5. It was a hospital for leprous maidens.
6. She travelled the equivalent of seventeen times round the world.

213

1. The colour was specially blended to go with her crimson and purple robes.
2. The 'thinking man's princess', the 'beautiful Sloane princess' and the 'Coronation Street princess'.
3. 'Ich dien' (I serve).
4. Twenty-two hours.
5. George V.
6. In China.

64

1. What decision of Princess Anne caused the Queen unhappiness?
2. What game do the Queen and Prince Philip often propose to put guests at their ease?
3. Which is the Queen's official residence in Scotland?
4. What potential disasters occurred on the morning of the Queen's marriage?
5. How did his doctors think Henry VIII caught venereal disease?
6. Where did Andrew joke to reporters, 'My name is Andrew Edwards, my father is a gentleman farmer and my mother doesn't work'?

139

1. What is the Queen's most valuable brooch?
2. How much did the scaled-down James Bond car given to Charles by his parents for his sixth birthday cost?
3. Why was the Queen furious with Diana after the 1985 State Opening of Parliament?
4. What was George VI's wedding present to the Queen and Prince Philip?
5. Who was the first monarch to have electric lights and a telephone?
6. What did President Truman's very old mother say to the young Queen when they met?

214

1. Which historical prince was the Queen's favourite as a girl?
2. Who said, 'I'm no angel but I'm no Bo-Peep either'?
3. When was Prince Andrew's first public appearance?
4. What did Princess Anne reply when reporters in New Mexico asked what she thought of Diana having given birth to a son?
5. Of whom did Harold Nicolson say, 'For seventeen years he did nothing at all but kill animals and stick in stamps'?
6. Where was Princess Alexandra's first solo official foreign tour?

64

1. Her insistence that her children should have no titles.
2. They invite them to think of a witty name for a new horse.
3. Holyrood House.
4. Her tiara broke, her pearls got mixed up with the wedding presents and her bouquet was mislaid.
5. When Cardinal Wolsey whispered in his ear.
6. In France.

139

1. A priceless piece incorporating the third and fourth parts of the Cullinan diamond.
2. Around £4000.
3. She chose that day to unveil her new hairstyle and the papers reported nothing else.
4. A Daimler limousine.
5. Queen Victoria.
6. 'I'm so glad your father's been re-elected.'

214

1. Bonnie Prince Charlie.
2. Princess Margaret.
3. On the Buckingham Palace balcony after the 1961 Trooping the Colour.
4. 'I didn't know she'd had one.'
5. George V.
6. Australia, 1959.

65

1. What did the Queen say to Maria Callas after watching her superb performance in *Tosca*?
2. What is the Queen Mother's full name?
3. What tune did the Grenadier Guards play on Prince Charles's fourth birthday?
4. What did well-wishing Americans send the Queen and Prince Philip as wedding presents?
5. Which monarch bought Sandringham House?
6. Where was Prince Philip based when serving in the Mediterranean Fleet?

140

1. What was the fourteen-year-old Queen's comment on being told of the outbreak of World War II?
2. Where did Princess Margaret hold her fiftieth birthday party?
3. Who was the first of the Princes and Peers to pay homage to the Queen after her Coronation?
4. How many guests attended the wedding of Charles and Diana in St Paul's?
5. How many bombs hit Buckingham Palace during World War II?
6. Which royal was given the name 'Soya Hun' by the Algonquin Indians?

215

1. How long did Fagin keep the Queen talking in her bedroom?
2. How old was Charles when he was voted one of the world's 'Top Ten Best Dressed Men'?
3. How does Prince Philip's position differ from that of Queen Victoria's husband, Albert?
4. Which childhood friend of Prince Philip is rumoured to have been his girlfriend?
5. What were George V's official last words?
6. Which royal attracted this headline in the USA, 'Here He Is Girls – the Most Eligible Bachelor Yet Uncaught?

65

1. 'What a pretty frock you're wearing.'
2. Elizabeth Angela Marguerite.
3. 'The Teddy Bear's Picnic'.
4. 32000 food parcels.
5. Edward VII.
6. Malta.

140

1. 'More history for children to learn in a hundred years' time.'
2. At the Ritz.
3. Prince Philip.
4. About 3500.
5. Nine.
6. Prince Andrew.

215

1. Ten minutes.
2. Four.
3. Prince Albert was Consort, Prince Philip is not.
4. Hélène Cordet.
5. 'How stands the Empire?'
6. The Duke of Windsor, on his 1924 tour of America.

66

1. Why was the Queen's Gallery created from the bombed Royal Chapel at Buckingham Palace?
2. Which members of the Royal Family have been fined for speeding?
3. Where did the Queen publicly announce her intention of creating Charles Prince of Wales?
4. Who was the first heir to the throne to be present at his child's birth?
5. Which Bishops traditionally carry the Paten, the Bible and the Chalice during the Coronation ceremony?
6. What revenge did the plumber take when Mrs Roosevelt refused to pay him for the new lavatory he'd installed for George VI's visit?

141

1. How many licences does the Queen hold for her numerous dogs?
2. What did Diana give Charles for his thirty-second birthday?
3. Which legendary pop star returned his MBE because he didn't believe in 'royalty and titles'?
4. Which royal lady proposed to her husband?
5. How did Elizabeth I punish the man who said she was too old to marry?
6. During which period could the British monarch also use the title Emperor of India?

216

1. What was the number plate of the car George VI bought the Queen for her eighteenth birthday?
2. Which of the Queen's sons poured foaming bath essence into Windsor Castle's swimming pool?
3. What name did Tony Armstrong-Jones give his first photographic exhibition?
4. How long did Margaret's romance with Townsend last?
5. Name four left-handed monarchs?
6. What extraordinary offer did a tightrope walker make to Edward VII during his 1860 visit to America?

66

1. The Queen wanted more people to enjoy the royal art treasures.
2. Princess Anne and Mark Phillips.
3. At the closing of the Empire and Commonwealth Games in Cardiff.
4. Prince Charles.
5. The Bishops of London, Norwich and Winchester.
6. He put it in his shop window with a sign reading 'the King and Queen sat here'.

141

1. The Queen is not required to hold dog licences.
2. Two white shirts from Harrods.
3. John Lennon.
4. Queen Victoria.
5. She ordered his right hand to be cut off.
6. 1877–1947.

216

1. JGY 280.
2. Prince Andrew.
3. 'Photocall'.
4. Twelve years.
5. James I, George II, George IV, George VI.
6. To push him across a rope over the Niagara Falls in a wheelbarrow.

67

1. What is the exclusive royal decoration worn by the Queen and her female relatives?
2. Of whom was it said, 'That little woman has grounds for a libel suit every time her picture is taken'?
3. Which three princesses watched Charles being formally introduced to the House of Lords?
4. When is Prince Philip said to have given up smoking?
5. Name four second sons who succeeded to the throne?
6. What country did Diana visit on her first solo official trip abroad?

142

1. Who said the Queen is the only person who can put on a tiara with one hand while walking down stairs?
2. Why did Princess Anne's adored horse Doublet have to be destroyed?
3. Which were Tony's first official pictures of Margaret?
4. On what date was Charles and Diana's engagement announced?
5. Name two puddings named after George III's wife, Charlotte.
6. What was the total value of the gifts received by the Queen during her 1979 Gulf tour?

217

1. Name the Queen's horse that won the Prix de Diane in 1974?
2. Who was the hairdresser who gave Diana her most copied style?
3. How long did the Royal Family TV film take to make?
4. What did the Queen reply when asked if she was nervous about having a baby?
5. Which member of the Royal Family was born on the anniversary of Prince Albert's death?
6. What would have happened to the principality of Monaco if Prince Rainier had failed to produce a son?

67

1. The 'Family Order'.
2. The young Queen Mother (because no picture could do justice to her beauty).
3. Princess Anne, Princess Margaret, Princess Alexandra.
4. The night before his wedding.
5. Henry VIII, Charles I, George V, George VI.
6. Oslo, 1984.

142

1. Princess Margaret.
2. He broke a leg.
3. The ones he took for her twenty-ninth birthday.
4. 24 February 1981.
5. 'Apple Charlotte' and 'Charlotte Russe'.
6. Over £1 million.

217

1. Highclere.
2. Kevin Shanley.
3. Seventy-five days.
4. 'It's what we're made for.'
5. George VI.
6. It would have reverted to France.

68

1. How much did the Queen pay for her daughter's house, Gatcombe Park?
2. At what age was Charles given his bachelor suite in Buckingham Palace?
3. What do the Queen and her husband regard as the turning point of the reign?
4. Who was Prince Charles's best man?
5. Who was the last King of America?
6. What is the name of Margaret's Mustique home?

143

1. Which of the Queen's ladies-in-waiting is an American from Rhode Island?
2. Which two members of the Royal Family were born on Christmas Day?
3. Which Duke masterminded the Queen's Coronation?
4. Who was the first heir apparent to publicly kiss his wife on Buckingham Palace's balcony.
5. To what use were the lawns and golf course at Sandringham put during World War II?
6. What food will the Queen and Prince Philip *not* eat when abroad?

218

1. Which is the only home the Queen actually owns in England?
2. Who said, 'I may be a lot of things, but I'm not boring'?
3. What did Lord Snowdon design for London Zoo?
4. Which of Princess Margaret's admirers committed suicide?
5. Of which Scottish king is the Queen Mother a direct descendant?
6. Where did Princess Anne spend her sixteenth birthday?

68

1. Around £700,000.
2. At twenty-one.
3. The initiation of the Queen's walk-abouts.
4. He didn't have one. He had two 'supporters', Prince Andrew and Prince Edward.
5. George III.
6. Les Jolies Eaux.

143

1. The Countess of Airlie.
2. Princess Alice, Duchess of Gloucester and Princess Alexandra.
3. The sixteenth Duke of Norfolk.
4. Prince Charles.
5. They were used for food production.
6. Seafood – they cannot risk being ill.

218

1. Sandringham House.
2. Princess Michael.
3. The aviary.
4. Robin Douglas-Home.
5. Robert II.
6. In Jamaica attending the Commonwealth Games.

69

1. What is the Queen's passport number and what is Philip's?
2. Who made up the winning team in a clay pigeon shoot in aid of the Save the Children Fund?
3. When did the Queen create Philip an English Prince?
4. What did Anne do with most of the money she received from the Services as a wedding present?
5. What final gesture did James I make before going into exile in 1689?
6. Where was the Queen carried ashore in a canoe by twenty-six half-naked islanders?

144

1. What law did the Queen obey on her sixteenth birthday?
2. Who said, 'I've learnt the way a monkey learns, by watching its parents'?
3. What was Prince Philip's title before he married the Queen?
4. What was the one characteristic that irritated George VI about his beloved wife?
5. How did George V like his trousers pressed?
6. Whom did Margaret Trudeau accuse of looking 'long and hard down my cleavage'?

219

1. What atmosphere does the Queen like in her private apartments?
2. When was Princess Margaret *Desert Island Discs*' 'Castaway of the Year'?
3. What are the Queen's 'nearest guard' called?
4. Which of Prince Charles's girlfriends modelled for a girlie magazine?
5. Who said, 'Every drop of blood in my veins is German'?
6. Farah Diba is a close friend of which member of the Royal Family?

69

1. The Queen does not need a passport. Philip's is No. 1.
2. Mark Phillips, Prince Andrew, The Duke of Kent and ex-King Constantine.
3. 22 February 1957.
4. She donated it to a charity for the mentally handicapped.
5. He dropped the Great Seal into the Thames.
6. Turalu, in the Pacific in 1982.

144

1. She registered at her local labour exchange.
2. Prince Charles.
3. Prince Philip of Greece and Denmark.
4. Her unpunctuality.
5. With no crease down the front.
6. Prince Charles.

219

1. She likes rooms to look 'really lived in'.
2. 1981.
3. The Honourable Corps of Gentlemen-at-Arms.
4. Fiona Watson.
5. The Duke of Windsor, to Diana Mosley.
6. The Queen Mother.

70

1. Who told the Queen they were both descended from the Prophet Mohammed?
2. Who has been called the 'first Royal Superstar'?
3. Who holds the titles of Earl of Merioneth and Baron Greenwich of Greenwich?
4. What were the birth weights of Charles, Anne, Andrew and Edward?
5. Who said, 'King George himself told me he would never have died had he had another doctor'?
6. To whom did the Queen apologize for the small size of an official gift?

145

1. When was the Queen christened and what are her full names?
2. Who said, 'I simply treat the press as though they were children'?
3. What drinks will the Queen accept at an official meal?
4. How many extra clothing coupons was the Queen granted for her wedding?
5. What diamond does the Royal Family possess that was described in 1526 as so valuable 'it would pay half the expenses of the world'?
6. Where did Princess Anne spend her nineteenth birthday?

220

1. What special snapshot of her husband does the Queen prize?
2. Who is Diana's favourite hat designer?
3. How long had Philip been in the Navy before getting his own command?
4. What did the Queen receive from the American people on the birth of Prince Charles?
5. What did Elizabeth I use to whiten her skin?
6. How many staff accompany the Queen on foreign tours?

70

1. Robert Graves.
2. Prince Andrew.
3. Prince Philip.
4. 7 lbs 6 oz, 6 lbs, 7lbs 3oz, 5lbs 7oz.
5. Asquith's wife, Margot.
6. To a sheikh's wife during the 1979 Gulf Tour.

145

1. 29 May 1926. Elizabeth Alexandra Mary.
2. Princess Diana.
3. One glass of red or white wine or orange juice.
4. 100. Her bridesmaids were given twenty-five each.
5. The Koh-i-Noor.
6. On the royal yacht *Bloodhound* on the Norwegian fiords.

220

1. A picture of Philip with a full carroty beard taken on his 1956 Antarctic trip.
2. John Boyd.
3. Twelve years.
4. They sent one and a half tons of nappies.
5. A mixture of egg, powdered eggshell, poppy seeds, lead, borax and alum.
6. Between forty-five and fifty.

71

1. What is the Queen's supreme racing ambition?
2. Which member of the Royal Family could hum *The Merry Widow* before she was one?
3. Which paper prints the Court Circular everyday?
4. From what station was the station master whom the Queen invited to her wedding?
5. Why was Mary Queen of Scots' Italian secretary stabbed to death in the tower of Holyrood House?
6. What was Margaret's verdict of her official visit to Morocco?

146

1. Who is the Queen's hairdresser?
2. Where was twenty-six-year-old Margaret placed on the list of 'Best Dressed Women'?
3. When did the Queen give Anne the exclusive Family Order?
4. When did Princess Michael win her fight to have her marriage recognized by the Roman Catholic Church?
5. What common ancestor do Charles and Diana share?
6. Where did Philip shock the nation by announcing that the Royal Family would 'shortly be in the red'?

221

1. What did the Queen say to the preacher who offered to send her a present of a book when she was a child?
2. What was the name of the pony given to Anne when she was twelve?
3. When did Prince Philip finally sit beside the Queen at the State Opening of Parliament?
4. How long had the Queen been married when she became pregnant?
5. Why did Charles I knight his dwarf Jeffrey Hudson?
6. What Order was stripped from Emperor Hirohito during World War II?

71

1. To win the Derby.
2. Princess Margaret.
3. The *Daily Telegraph*.
4. Wolferton, Norfolk – then the nearest station to Sandringham.
5. He was suspected by her husband of being her lover.
6. 'It was more like being kidnapped.'

146

1. Charles Martyn.
2. She tied with the Duchess of Windsor below Grace Kelly.
3. April 1969.
4. July 1983.
5. King James I.
6. On American television in 1969.

221

1. 'Not about God. I know all about him already.'
2. High Jinks.
3. 31 October 1967.
4. Three months.
5. For his usefulness in court intrigue and diplomacy.
6. The Order of the Garter.

72

1. When did the Queen make her first appearance on Buckingham Palace's balcony?
2. How has Prince Philip's electric London 'runabout' been described?
3. What motifs were embroidered into the Queen's Coronation gown?
4. Which of Margaret's loves sang a duet with Petula Clark on French TV?
5. What great treasure was ravaged in the 1891 fire at Sandringham?
6. In which science is Emperor Hirohito of Japan an authority?

147

1. How much did the Queen receive from the Civil List in 1977?
2. What fashion accessory is considered essential for all royal occasions?
3. How many engagements were undertaken by the Queen in her fortieth year?
4. When did Anne first kiss Mark Phillips in public?
5. Who gave Queen Victoria daily lessons in Hindustani?
6. To which countries did the Queen make State visits in 1957?

222

1. On what occasion did the Queen exclaim, 'Oh, Philip, do look. I've got my Miss Piggy face on!'?
2. How many cards and telegrams did the Queen Mother receive on her eightieth birthday?
3. Which Keeper of the Queen's Pictures was a Russian spy?
4. What line did Diana fluff in her marriage ceremony?
5. Which monarch was responsible for the Authorized Version of the Bible?
6. When did the Queen first visit Margaret's home on Mustique?

72

1. 27 June 1927, aged fourteen months.
2. As looking like an electric milk float.
3. The flower symbols representing the UK and the emblems of all the dominions of which she was Queen.
4. Roddy Llewellyn.
5. The Goya tapestries.
6. Marine biology.

147

1. £1,905,000.
2. Hats.
3. Over 500.
4. 1973, seeing him off to rejoin his regiment in Germany.
5. Her favoured Indian servant, Abdul Karim.
6. Portugal, France, Denmark, Canada and the USA.

222

1. Watching herself on the televized wedding-eve party for Charles and Diana.
2. 35,000.
3. Antony Blunt.
4. She muddled Charles's middle names.
5. James I.
6. November 1977.

73

1. When was the first time since childhood that the Queen wept over a horse?
2. Who called the Queen Mother the 'epitome of style'?
3. Why does the Queen use a special black blotting paper?
4. Who played gooseberry at the Queen's first proper encounter with Philip?
5. Which fat Queen's coffin was nearly twice as wide as it was long?
6. On which foreign tour did the Queen and Prince Philip use bullet-proof cars?

148

1. Which of her predecessors does the Queen most admire?
2. Which member of the Royal Family said, 'I've always wished I could heal'?
3. Which was the most difficult of the Silver Jubilee visits?
4. What specially significant hymn did the Duke and Duchess of Windsor arrange to be sung at their wedding?
5. Who said the famous line, 'We are not amused'?
6. Of how many independent countries is Elizabeth II Queen?

223

1. Name three contemporary painters the Queen privately collects?
2. Which member of the Royal Family has kept a dream diary?
3. Who is the Queen's private secretary?
4. Who was Princess Alexandra's chief bridesmaid?
5. What did a young suffragette sympathizer say when presented to George V?
6. Where was a concrete block thrown at the Queen's car?

73

1. 1956, when Doutelle died as a result of biting his neck-chain.
2. Sir Roy Strong, Director of the Victoria and Albert Museum.
3. To prevent private or state secrets from being revealed.
4. Nine-year-old Princess Margaret.
5. Queen Anne's.
6. On the 1984 visit to Jordan.

148

1. Queen Victoria.
2. Prince Charles.
3. The visit to Ulster.
4. 'O Perfect Love'.
5. Queen Victoria.
6. Seventeen.

223

1. Malcolm Lowry, Graham Sutherland and Alan Davie.
2. Prince Charles.
3. Sir Philip Moore.
4. Princess Anne.
5. 'Your Majesty, for God's sake stop torturing women!'
6. Belfast, 1966.

74

1. Until what age did the Queen share a room with 'Bobo' MacDonald?
2. What provoked the Duke of Norfolk to describe Snowdon as looking like a 'bell hop at a hotel'?
3. How much does the royal yacht *Britannia* cost the state every year?
4. Who was Charles's very first girlfriend?
5. What happens to the wand, symbol of the Lord Chamberlain's office, when a monarch dies?
6. What was the highest Japanese award that the Queen wore when Emperor Hirohito visited Britain?

149

1. What were the complications at the Queen's birth?
2. Where did Princess Anne tell reporters to 'naff off!'?
3. Describe the tie of the Royal Household social club?
4. Where was it falsely rumoured that Charles and Diana had spent an illicit night of unwedded love?
5. What did George VI die of?
6. Why was Emperor Hirohito's 1971 State Visit to Britain historical?

224

1. Which three periodicals does the Queen read regularly?
2. Who said, 'I'm very humble mumble, "Yes Ma'am, no Ma'am in the corner"'?
3. Which member of the present Royal Family has exhibited at the Royal Academy?
4. Princess Margaret was forty-three when she met Roddy Llewellyn. How old was he?
5. Why did Queen Mary abolish maids-of-honour?
6. Who described the Queen as a 'very interesting lady with a lot of savvy'?

74

1. Until she was eleven.
2. His outfit for the Investiture of Prince Charles.
3. Over £3.5 million.
4. Lucia Santa Cruz, daughter of the Chilean ambassador.
5. It's broken at the end of the funeral service.
6. The Grand Cordon of the Order of the Chrysanthemum.

149

1. She was a breech baby and had to be delivered by caesarean section.
2. At the Badminton Horse Trials, 1982.
3. It has navy blue, maroon and thin gold stripes.
4. In the carriage of the royal train parked in the West Country.
5. Lung cancer.
6. It was the first trip outside Japan ever undertaken by a reigning Japanese sovereign.

224

1. *Sporting Life*, the *Daily Telegraph* and *The Times*.
2. Princess Michael.
3. Prince Philip.
4. Twenty-five.
5. To save on their dowries.
6. Henry Kissinger.

75

1. Who is the Queen's senior lady-in-waiting?
2. What did Princess Margaret do when a bottle of rare vodka went missing from her house after a party?
3. What flag is flown when the Queen is on the *Britannia*?
4. How long was Diana's wedding train?
5. Who was the first member of the Royal Family to be born in Scotland for 300 years?
6. What new skill did Charles acquire during his Jubilee tour of the USA?

150

1. To what institution is the Queen most ardently devoted?
2. Which members of the Royal Family were at the seance where medium Lilian Bailey contacted the spirit of George VI?
3. Who is Prince Charles's private secretary?
4. How many state rooms in St James's Palace were required to display the Queen's and Prince Philip's wedding presents?
5. What is the hereditary duty of the Duke of Norfolk?
6. Why did the Duke of Windsor have to bandage his right hand when he toured Australia as King?

225

1. How often does the Queen phone her mother?
2. Where does the Royal Family spend New Year?
3. How old was Prince Charles when he won the Duke of Edinburgh's Award Scheme silver medal?
4. Who made the slippers Diana wore on her wedding day?
5. How did James I try to cure his rheumatic feet?
6. What political tragedy occurred during Princess Anne's 1984 tour of India?

75

1. The Duchess of Grafton.
2. She telephoned every guest to unmask the culprit.
3. The flag of the Lord High Admiral.
4. Twenty-five feet.
5. Princess Margaret.
6. Cattle driving.

150

1. The Commonwealth.
2. The Queen Mother, the Queen, Princess Alexandra, the Duchess of Kent, Prince Philip.
3. Edward Adeane.
4. Five.
5. To stage-manage all principal ceremonies.
6. His hand became sore and swollen from so many handshakes.

225

1. Several times a day.
2. Sandringham.
3. Seventeen.
4. Clive Shelton.
5. By thrusting them into the bellies of newly slaughtered bucks.
6. Mrs Gandhi was assassinated.

FOR THE BEST IN PAPERBACKS, LOOK FOR THE

In every corner of the world, on every subject under the sun, Penguin represents quality and variety – the very best in publishing today.

For complete information about books available from Penguin – including Pelicans, Puffins, Peregrines and Penguin Classics – and how to order them, write to us at the appropriate address below. Please note that for copyright reasons the selection of books varies from country to country.

In the United Kingdom: For a complete list of books available from Penguin in the U.K., please write to *Dept E.P., Penguin Books Ltd, Harmondsworth, Middlesex, UB7 0DA*

In the United States: For a complete list of books available from Penguin in the U.S., please write to *Dept BA, Penguin, 299 Murray Hill Parkway, East Rutherford, New Jersey 07073*

In Canada: For a complete list of books available from Penguin in Canada, please write to *Penguin Books Canada Ltd, 2801 John Street, Markham, Ontario L3R 1B4*

In Australia: For a complete list of books available from Penguin in Australia, please write to the *Marketing Department, Penguin Books Australia Ltd, P.O. Box 257, Ringwood, Victoria 3134*

In New Zealand: For a complete list of books available from Penguin in New Zealand, please write to the *Marketing Department, Penguin Books (NZ) Ltd, Private Bag, Takapuna, Auckland 9*

In India: For a complete list of books available from Penguin, please write to *Penguin Overseas Ltd, 706 Eros Apartments, 56 Nehru Place, New Delhi, 110019*

In Holland: For a complete list of books available from Penguin in Holland, please write to *Penguin Books Nederland B.V., Postbus 195, NL–1380AD Weesp, Netherlands*

In Germany: For a complete list of books available from Penguin, please write to *Penguin Books Ltd, Friedrichstrasse 10 – 12, D–6000 Frankfurt Main 1, Federal Republic of Germany*

In Spain: For a complete list of books available from Penguin in Spain, please write to *Longman Penguin España, Calle San Nicolas 15, E–28013 Madrid, Spain*

A CHOICE OF PENGUINS

The Book Quiz Book   Joseph Connolly

Who was literature's performing flea . . .? Who wrote 'Live Now, Pay Later . . .'? Keats and Cartland, Balzac and Braine, Coleridge conundrums, Eliot enigmas, Tolstoy teasers . . . all in this brilliant quiz book. You will be on the shelf without it . . .

Voyage through the Antarctic   Richard Adams and Ronald Lockley

Here is the true, authentic Antarctic of today, brought vividly to life by Richard Adams, author of *Watership Down*, and Ronald Lockley, the world-famous naturalist. 'A good adventure story, with a lot of information and a deal of enthusiasm for Antarctica and its animals' – *Nature*

Getting to Know the General   Graham Greene

'In August 1981 my bag was packed for my fifth visit to Panama when the news came to me over the telephone of the death of General Omar Torrijos Herrera, my friend and host . . .' 'Vigorous, deeply felt, at times funny, and for Greene surprisingly frank' – *Sunday Times*

Television Today and Tomorrow: Wall to Wall Dallas?
Christopher Dunkley

Virtually every British home has a television, nearly half now have two sets or more, and we are promised that before the end of the century there will be a vast expansion of television delivered via cable and satellite. How did television come to be so central to our lives? Is British television really the best in the world, as politicians like to assert?

Arabian Sands   Wilfred Thesiger

'In the tradition of Burton, Doughty, Lawrence, Philby and Thomas, it is, very likely, the book about Arabia to end all books about Arabia' – *Daily Telegraph*

When the Wind Blows   Raymond Briggs

'A visual parable against nuclear war: all the more chilling for being in the form of a strip cartoon' – *Sunday Times*. 'The most eloquent anti-Bomb statement you are likely to read' – *Daily Mail*

A CHOICE OF PENGUINS

A Fortunate Grandchild 'Miss Read'

Grandma Read in Lewisham and Grandma Shafe in Walton on the Naze were totally different in appearance and outlook, but united in their affection for their grand-daughter – who grew up to become the much-loved and popular novelist.

The Ultimate Trivia Quiz Game Book Maureen and Alan Hiron

If you are immersed in trivia, addicted to quiz games, endlessly nosey, then this is the book for you: over 10,000 pieces of utterly dispensable information!

The Diary of Virginia Woolf
Five volumes, edited by Quentin Bell and Anne Olivier Bell

'As an account of the intellectual and cultural life of our century, Virginia Woolf's diaries are invaluable; as the record of one bruised and unquiet mind, they are unique'– Peter Ackroyd in the *Sunday Times*

Voices of the Old Sea Norman Lewis

'I will wager that *Voices of the Old Sea* will be a classic in the literature about Spain' – *Mail on Sunday*. 'Limpidly and lovingly Norman Lewis has caught the helpless, unwitting, often foolish, but always hopeful village in its dying summers, and saved the tragedy with sublime comedy' – *Observer*

The First World War A. J. P. Taylor

In this superb illustrated history, A. J. P. Taylor 'manages to say almost everything that is important for an understanding and, indeed, intellectual digestion of that vast event . . . A special text . . . a remarkable collection of photographs' – *Observer*

Ninety-Two Days Evelyn Waugh

With characteristic honesty, Evelyn Waugh here debunks the romantic notions attached to rough travelling: his journey in Guiana and Brazil is difficult, dangerous and extremely uncomfortable, and his account of it is witty and unquestionably compelling.